SUMMER COOKING

**Recipes Compiled by Judith Ferguson
and Beverley Piper
Photography by Peter Barry
Designed by Philip Clucas**

2691
This edition published 1993 by Coombe Books
© 1991 CLB Publishing, Godalming, Surrey
Printed and bound in Singapore by Tien Wah Press
ISBN 0 86283 874 6

SUMMER COOKING

COOMBE BOOKS

SUMMER COOKING

CONTENTS

INTRODUCTION

Warm, hazy days and long tranquil evenings herald the arrival of summer, bringing with it a new season of relaxed, al fresco eating. Summer provides an abundance of colourful and delicious ingredients to inspire the cook, and the hearty stews and roasts of winter are forgotten in favour of lunches in the garden and the delights of picnics and barbecues.

The growing popularity of barbecues means that almost every household indulges in the yearly ritual of producing the barbecue at the first hint of sun. Barbecued food has a unique taste which endears it to all age groups – children love the fun of chicken drumsticks and kebabs, whilst adults can enjoy the unique taste of dishes such as Orange Grilled Duck or Javanese Pork. There is no reason why the barbecue cannot progress to being more than just a celebration of the sausage and burger! Cooking exciting food on a barbecue is something anyone can learn and adapt to their own tastes.

The huge range of barbecues available means that cooking times for barbecued foods cannot be very exact. There is room for variation depending on the type of grill and source of heat. For grills without adjustable shelves, results are better if the food is cooked in the oven for about half to three-quarters of the cooking time and the remaining time on the barbecue grill for colour and flavour. Similarly, larger cuts of meat such as Butterflied Lamb will cook faster and be juicier if pre-cooked in the oven. In fact, employ this method with any food cooked for a large group and you will avoid the problem of eating in shifts. The use of the barbecue for grilling vegetables is often overlooked. Barbecued vegetables such as Grilled Fennel or Courgette, Pepper and Onion Kebabs are delicious and are sure to impress your guests.

Salads are the natural choice for outdoor meals. Summer salads are light, colourful and full of goodness and within these pages you will find an enticing range of recipes from main course salads such as Hungarian Sausage Salad, to the perfect side salads for barbecued meats. The addition of the unusual ingredient can lift any salad out of the ordinary, consequently the days of the simple lettuce , tomato and cucumber salad are numbered. The warm summer months mean smaller appetites and lighter more delicate foods, and one of the great delights of entertaining during this time of the year is the way in which convention can be thrown to the wind. Summer eating means a whole range of appetizers, dips, salads and vegetables can be joined together in one enticing, nutritious feast. Cold soups in particular are a delightfully refreshing start to a meal and many only need the briefest preparation, Avocado Cream Soup is a perfect example.

The ultimate summer delight often comes in the shape of a dessert. A whole array of delightful fruits are at their best in the summer and can be utilized in a wondrous array of delectable desserts. Ice creams and sorbets are also at their most tempting on warm nights and are the perfect finale for a barbecue or sophisticated main course salad.

Summer is the perfect time for entertaining, and large numbers of guests are often best catered for by an enticing array of party snacks. These can very often be prepared in advance and offer unlimited opportunities for the ingenious use of a whole range of ingredients. Gone are the days of cocktail sticks, vol-au-vents and sausage rolls, now you can replace them with a tempting spread, including Avocado Cheese Balls, Smoked Salmon Flowers, Stuffed Mushrooms and Chinese Melon, to name but a few. *Summer Cooking* also features a section on mocktails, which give all the taste of a cocktail without the alcohol. These drinks are perfect for summer entertaining and are especially appreciated by guests who drive!

Summer Cooking offers endless scope for every cook and with an enticing range of recipes to suit all occasions you will have the means to create the most delicious of summer feasts.

BARBECUED APPETIZERS AND SIDE SALADS

Satay

PREPARATION TIME: 25 minutes

COOKING TIME: 10-15 minutes

SERVES: 4 people

450g/1lb chicken, skinned, boned and cut into 2.5cm/1 inch cubes

MARINADE
30ml/2 tbsps soy sauce
30ml/2 tbsps oil
30ml/2 tbsps lime juice
5ml/1 tsp ground cumin
5ml/1 tsp turmeric
10ml/2 tsps ground coriander

SAUCE
30ml/2 tbsps oil
1 small onion, finely chopped
5ml/1 tsp chili powder
120g/4oz/1 cup peanut butter
5ml/1 tsp brown sugar
Remaining marinade

GARNISH
Lime wedges
Coriander leaves

Combine the marinade ingredients in a deep bowl. Put in the meat and stir to coat. Leave covered in the refrigerator for 1 hour. Drain and thread the meat on 4 large or 8 small skewers. Grill about 10-15 minutes, turning frequently to cook all sides. Baste often. Meanwhile heat the oil in a small saucepan. Add the onion and the chili powder. Cook until the onion is slightly softened. Take off the heat and set aside. When the meat is nearly cooked combine the marinade with the oil and onion and chili powder. Stir in the remaining sauce ingredients, thinning with water if necessary. Brush the Satay with the sauce 1 to 2 minutes before the end of cooking time. Spoon over a bit more sauce and serve the rest separately. Garnish each serving with lime wedges and coriander leaves.

This page: **Rumaki (left) and Satay (right). Facing page: Grilled Garlic Prawns/Shrimp (left) aand Smoked Fish Kebabs with Horseradish Sauce (right).**

Rumaki

PREPARATION TIME: 15 minutes

COOKING TIME: 10-15 minutes

SERVES: 4 people

180ml/6 fl oz/¾ cup soy sauce
450g/1lb chicken livers, trimmed and cut
 into 5cm/2 inch pieces
1 200g/7oz can water chestnuts, drained
8 slices smoked streaky bacon
1 red pepper, cut in 2.5cm/1 inch pieces
Brown sugar

Combine half the soy sauce and all the chicken livers in a deep bowl. Leave to marinate in the refrigerator for 1 hour. Place the bacon slices on a wooden board. Stretch the bacon by running the back of knife backwards and forwards over each slice. Cut the slices in half across. Drain the chicken livers and discard the soy sauce. Put a piece of liver and a water chestnut on each slice of bacon and roll up. Thread on skewers, alternating with a piece of red pepper. Grill on an oiled rack above hot coals for 10-15 minutes, basting with the remaining half of the soy sauce and turning frequently. One minute before the end of cooking, sprinkle lightly with brown sugar and allow to glaze. Garnish serving dishes with parsley if desired.

Greek Salad

PREPARATION TIME: 15 minutes

SERVES: 4 people

1 head cos/romaine lettuce
16 black olives, stoned
120g/4oz/1 cup crumbled feta cheese
1 small can anchovies, drained
8 mild pickled peppers
60g/2oz cherry tomatoes, halved
½ cucumber, cut in small dice
30ml/2 tbsps chopped fresh oregano or
 15ml/1 tbsp dried oregano

DRESSING
120ml/4 fl oz/½ cup olive oil
45ml/3 tbsps red wine vinegar
1 clove garlic, finely minced
Salt and pepper

Wash and dry the cos/romaine lettuce and tear the leaves into bite-size pieces. Place the leaves in a large salad bowl and arrange or scatter all the other ingredients on top of the lettuce. If the anchovies are large, cut them into thinner strips or chop into small pieces. Sprinkle the fresh or dried oregano over all the ingredients in the salad bowl. Mix the dressing together well and pour over the salad just before serving.

Caesar Salad

PREPARATION TIME: 20 minutes

COOKING TIME: 3 minutes

SERVES: 4-6 people

1 large or two small heads cos/romaine
 lettuce
8 slices white bread, crusts removed
120ml/4 fl oz/½ cup oil
1 clove garlic, peeled
1 small can anchovies
90g/3oz fresh Parmesan cheese

DRESSING
1 egg
120ml/4 fl oz/½ cup olive oil
Juice of 1 lemon
1 clove garlic, finely minced
Salt and pepper

Wash the lettuce and dry well. Tear the lettuce into bite-size pieces and place in a large salad bowl, or four individual bowls. Cut the slices of bread into 1.25cm/½ inch dice. Heat the vegetable oil in a small frying pan. When the oil is hot put in the clove of garlic and the cubes of bread. Lower the heat slightly and, using a metal spoon, keep stirring the cubes of bread to brown them evenly. When they are golden brown and crisp, remove them to paper towels to drain. Add the anchovies to the lettuce in the salad bowl and sprinkle on the fried bread croûtons. To prepare the dressing, place the egg in boiling water for 1 minute. Break into a small bowl and combine with remaining dressing ingredients, whisking very well. Pour the dressing over the salad and toss. Using a cheese slicer, shave off thin slices of Parmesan cheese and add to the salad. Alternatively, grate the cheese and add to the salad with the dressing.

Smoked Fish Kebabs with Horseradish Sauce

PREPARATION TIME: 15 minutes

COOKING TIME: 6 minutes

SERVES: 4 people

1 smoked kipper fillet, skinned and cut
 into 2.5cm/1 inch pieces
1 smoked haddock fillet, skinned and cut
 into 2.5cm/1 inch pieces
8 bay leaves
1 small red onion, quartered
Oil
SAUCE
30ml/2 tbsps grated fresh or bottled
 horseradish
280ml/½ pint/1 cup sour cream
10ml/2 tsps fresh dill, chopped
Salt and pepper
Squeeze of lemon juice
Pinch sugar

Thread the fish, bay leaves and slices of onion on skewers, alternating ingredients and types of fish. Brush with oil and place on an oiled grill rack above hot coals. Mix the sauce ingredients together and divide onto side plates. Grill the kebabs for about 6 minutes, turning and basting with oil frequently. When the onion is cooked, remove to serving dishes. Place kebabs on lettuce leaves, if desired, for serving.

Grilled Garlic Prawns/ Shrimp

PREPARATION TIME: 15 minutes

COOKING TIME: 8-10 minutes

SERVES: 4 people

900g/2lbs uncooked king prawns/jumbo
 shrimp
60g/2oz/4 tbsps melted butter

Facing page: Greek Salad (top) and Caesar Salad (bottom).

30ml/2 tbsps double/heavy cream
Salt and pepper
15ml/1 tbsp sugar

Place the carrots in iced water for 1 hour. Dry them and grate coarsely into a bowl. Add the raisins, nuts and sesame seeds. Mix the dressing ingredients together, adding more cream if the dressing appears too thick. If dressing separates, whisk vigorously until it comes together before adding additional cream. Toss with the carrot salad and serve.

Curried Rice Salad

PREPARATION TIME: 20 minutes

COOKING TIME: 12 minutes

SERVES: 6 people

180g/6oz/¾ cup long grain rice
15ml/1 tbsp curry powder, hot or mild as desired
4 spring/green onions, sliced
2 sticks celery, sliced
1 small green pepper, diced
10 black olives, halved and stoned
60g/2oz/¼ cup sultanas/golden raisins
60g/2oz/¼ cup toasted flaked/sliced almonds
60ml/4 tbsps flaked coconut
2 hard-boiled eggs, chopped

DRESSING
140ml/¼ pint/½ cup mayonnaise
15ml/1 tbsp mango chutney
Juice and grated rind of ½ a lime
60ml/4 tbsps natural yogurt
Salt

GARNISH
2 avocados, peeled and cut in cubes
Juice of ½ lemon or lime

Cook the rice in boiling salted water for about 12 minutes or until tender. During the last 3 minutes of cooking time drain away half the water and stir in the curry powder. Leave to continue cooking over a gentle heat until the rice is cooked and the water

MARINADE
3 cloves garlic, finely chopped
60ml/4 tbsps oil
120ml/4 fl oz/½ cup lemon juice
60ml/4 tbsps chopped basil
Salt
Coarsely ground black pepper

Shell and de-vein the prawns/shrimp. Leave the shell on the ends of the tails. Combine the marinade ingredients in a plastic bag. Put in the prawns/shrimp and seal the bag. Refrigerate for 1 hour, turning frequently. Place the bag in a bowl to catch possible drips. Drain the prawns/shrimp and thread onto 4 skewers. Mix the marinade with the melted butter and brush the prawns/shrimp with the mixture. Grill for 8-10 minutes about 10-15cm/4-6

inches above the coals. Brush frequently with the marinade while the prawns/shrimp cook. Pour over remaining marinade before serving.

Carrot Salad with Creamy Sesame Dressing

PREPARATION TIME: 1 hour

SERVES: 4 people

4 large carrots, peeled
120g/4oz/1 cup raisins
120g/4oz/1 cup chopped walnuts
30ml/2 tbsps sesame seeds
30ml/2 tbsps oil
15ml/1 tbsp lemon juice
90ml/6 tbsps sesame paste (tahini)
90ml/6 tbsps warm water

This page: Carrot Salad with Creamy Sesame Dressing. Facing page: Curried Rice Salad.

is evaporated. Leave covered to stand for about 5 minutes. Toss the rice with a fork, drain away any excess water and leave to cool. Combine with the remaining salad ingredients, stirring carefully so that the hard-boiled eggs do not break up. Mix the dressing ingredients together thoroughly. Chop any large pieces of mango in the chutney finely. Stir the dressing into the salad and toss gently to coat. Arrange the rice salad in a mound on a serving dish. Sprinkle the cubed avocado with the lemon juice to keep it green and place around the rice salad before serving.

Cheese and Vine Leaves

PREPARATION TIME: 20 minutes

COOKING TIME: 6 minutes

SERVES: 4 people

4 pieces goat's, feta or haloumi cheese
280ml/½ pint/1 cup olive oil
60ml/4 tbsps chopped fresh herbs such as basil, tarragon, oregano, marjoram, parsley
2 cloves garlic, peeled and crushed (optional)
1 bay leaf
Squeeze lemon juice

TO SERVE
4 fresh vine leaves, washed, or 4 brine-packed vine leaves, soaked 30 minutes
1 head radicchio
8 leaves curly endive, washed and torn in bite-size pieces

If using goat's cheese, make sure it is not too ripe. Lightly score the surface of whichever cheese is used. Mix together the oil, herbs, garlic and lemon juice. Place the cheese in a small, deep bowl or jar and pour over the oil mixture. If cheese is not completely covered, pour on more oil. Leave, covered, overnight in the refrigerator. Drain the cheese and place in a hinged wire rack. Grill the cheese over hot coals until light golden brown and just beginning to melt. Drain and dry the vine leaves. Wash the radicchio and break apart the leaves. Arrange radicchio and endive leaves on 4 small plates and

place a vine leaf on top. Place the cooked cheese on top of the vine leaf and spoon some of the oil mixutre over each serving.

Gorgonzola and Bean Salad with Pine Nuts

PREPARATION TIME: 20 minutes

COOKING TIME: 4-5 minutes

SERVES: 4 people

340g/12oz French/green beans, ends trimmed
60g/2oz/½ cup pine nuts, toasted if desired
120g/4oz/1 cup crumbled gorgonzola or other blue cheese
30ml/2 tbsps red wine vinegar
90ml/6 tbsps olive oil
½ clove garlic, finely minced
Salt and pepper
2 heads radicchio

This page: **Cheese and Vine Leaves. Facing page: Gorgonzola and Bean Salad with Pine Nuts (top), and Spinach Salad with Bacon, Hazelnuts and Mushrooms (bottom).**

If the beans are large, cut across in half or thirds. Place in boiling salted water and cook for 4-5 minutes or until tender-crisp. Rinse under cold water and leave to drain. Toast pine nuts, if desired, at 180°C, 350°F, Gas Mark 4 for 10 minutes. Allow to cool. Mix the vinegar, oil, garlic, salt and pepper until well emulsified. Toss the beans in the dressing and add the cheese and nuts. Separate the leaves of radicchio, wash and dry. Arrange on salad plates and spoon the bean salad on top. Alternatively, tear radicchio into bite-size pieces and toss all the ingredients together.

Beetroot and Celeriac Salad

PREPARATION TIME: 25 minutes

COOKING TIME: 20 minutes

SERVES: 4 people

1 large celeriac root, peeled
4-6 cooked beets/beetroot
4 spring/green onions chopped
Juice of ½ a lemon

DRESSING
430ml/¾ pint/1½ cups sour cream
10ml/2 tsps white wine vinegar
Pinch sugar
10ml/2 tsps celery seed
25ml/1½ tbsps parsley

Cut the celeriac into 1.25cm/½ inch dice. Cook in boiling salted water with the juice of half a lemon for about 20 minutes or until tender. Drain and set aside to cool. Dice the beets/beetroot the same size as the celeriac. Mix the beets/beetroot with the spring/green onions and carefully combine with the celeriac. Mix the dressing ingredients together, reserving half of the parsley. Combine the dressing with the celeriac and the beets/beetroot, taking care not to over mix. Sprinkle the remaining parsley over the salad before serving.

Parsley Salad Vinaigrette

PREPARATION TIME: 20 minutes

COOKING TIME: 2 minutes

SERVES: 4 people

2 large bunches parsley (preferably flat Italian variety)
225g/8oz tomatoes, quartered and seeded
120g/4oz/1 cup stoned black olives, sliced
140ml/¼ pint/½ cup vegetable oil
1 clove garlic, finely minced
45ml/3 tbsps white wine vinegar
5ml/1 tsp dry mustard
Pinch sugar
Salt and pepper
60g/2oz/½ cup grated fresh Parmesan cheese

This page: Red Cabbage, Celery and Carrot Salad. Facing page: Parsley Salad Vinaigrette (top), and Beetroot and Celeriac Salad (bottom).

Pick over the parsley and discard any yellow and thick stems. Break parsley into individual leaves. Cut the tomatoes into 1.25cm/½ inch dice. Use 30ml/2 tbsps of measured oil and heat in a small frying pan. Add the finely chopped garlic and cook slowly to brown lightly. Combine with the remaining oil, vinegar, mustard, sugar, salt and pepper and beat well. Toss the dressing with the parsley, tomatoes and olives before serving. Sprinkle over the Parmesan cheese.

Red Cabbage, Celery and Carrot Salad

PREPARATION TIME: 15 minutes

SERVES: 6-8 people

1 small head red cabbage
4-6 carrots, peeled
4-6 sticks celery

DRESSING
120ml/4 fl oz/½ cup oil
15ml/1 tbsp white wine vinegar
30ml/2 tbsps lemon juice
15ml/1 tbsp honey
15ml/1 tbsp celery seed
10ml/2 tsps chopped parsley
Salt and pepper

Cut the cabbage in quarters and remove the core. Grate coarsely or

slice finely. Grate the carrots coarsely. Cut the celery into very fine strips. Combine all the vegetables in a large salad bowl or in individual bowls. Mix the salad dressing ingredients very well. This can be done by hand with wire whisk or in a blender. Once the dressing is well emulsified, add the celery seeds and whisk again. Pour over the salad and toss before serving.

Three Bean Salad

PREPARATION TIME: 15 minutes, plus marinating time

SERVES: 6-8 people

1 225g/8oz can chickpeas
1 225g/8oz can red kidney beans
1 225g/8oz can green flageolet beans
6-8 tomatoes, quartered

DRESSING
140ml/¼ pint/½ cup olive oil and
*   vegetable oil mixed*
60ml/4 tbsps white wine vinegar
30ml/2 tbsps chopped parsley
15ml/1 tbsp chopped basil
1 shallot, finely chopped
1 clove garlic, finely minced
Salt and pepper

Drain and rinse all the beans. Mix the dressing ingredients together thoroughly and combine with the beans. Allow to marinate for 2 hours. Mound the beans into a serving dish and surround with the quartered tomatoes to serve.

Pea, Cheese and Bacon Salad

PREPARATION TIME: 20 minutes

COOKING TIME: 15-20 minutes

SERVES: 6 people

6 strips bacon/smoked streaky bacon,
*   rind and bones removed*
450g/1lb fresh or frozen shelled peas
120g/4oz Red Leicester/Colby cheese
4 sticks celery, diced
4 spring/green onions, sliced thinly or
*   1 small red onion, diced*
1 red pepper, cored, seeded and diced

1 head Buttercrunch lettuce
180ml/6 fl oz/¾ cup sour cream or
*   natural yogurt*
15ml/1 tbsp chopped fresh mixed herbs
5ml/1 tsp white wine vinegar
5ml/1 tsp sugar
Salt and pepper

Dice the bacon and cook gently in a small frying pan until the fat runs. Turn up the heat and fry the bacon until brown and crisp. Remove to paper towels to drain. Meanwhile cook the peas in boiling salted water for 15-20 minutes for fresh peas and 5 minutes for frozen peas. When the peas are cooked, drain and refresh under cold water and leave to drain dry. Cut the cheese into dice slightly larger than the peas. Dice the celery and red pepper to the same size as

This page: Tomato and Mozzarella Salad with Fresh Basil. Facing page: Three Bean Salad (left), and Pea, Cheese and Bacon Salad (right).

the cheese. Combine the peas, cheese, celery, spring/green onions, red pepper and bacon in a bowl. Mix the dressing ingredients together, reserving half of the chopped mixed herbs. Combine the vegetables and bacon with half of the dressing. Separate the leaves of the lettuce and wash well. Pat dry and arrange on serving dishes. Spoon on the salad mixture and top with the remaining dressing. Sprinkle the reserved chopped herbs on top of the dressing.

Tomato and Mozzarella Salad with Fresh Basil

PREPARATION TIME: 15 minutes

SERVES: 4 people

3 large beefsteak tomatoes, sliced 6mm/
¼ inch thick
180g/6oz mozzarella cheese, drained,
dried and sliced 6mm/¼ inch thick
60ml/4 tbsps coarsely chopped fresh basil
leaves

DRESSING
90ml/6 tbsps olive oil and vegetable oil
mixed
30ml/2 tbsps balsamic vinegar or white
wine vinegar
1.25ml/¼ tsp Dijon mustard
Salt and pepper

GARNISH
Fresh basil leaves

Arrange the tomato slices and
mozzarella cheese slices in
overlapping circles on four individual
salad plates. Sprinkle the fresh
chopped basil leaves on top and
garnish in the centre with the whole
basil leaves. Mix all the dressing
ingredients together very well and
spoon some over the salads before
serving. Serve the rest of the dressing
separately.

Cracked Wheat Salad

PREPARATION TIME: 20 minutes

SERVES: 4-6 people

225g/8oz/2 cups bulgur wheat, washed
and drained
4 spring/green onions, chopped
1 cucumber, cut in small cubes
Juice and rind of 1 lemon
4 tomatoes, cubed
4 sticks celery, diced
60g/2oz/½ cup toasted sunflower seeds
120g/4oz/1 cup crumbled feta cheese
140ml/¼ pint/½ cup olive oil
1 clove garlic, minced
Salt and pepper
60ml/4 tbsps chopped mixed herbs

Place the washed bulgur wheat in
clean water and leave to soak for

5 minutes. Drain and squeeze as
much moisture out as possible.
Spread the wheat out onto a clean
towel to drain and dry. When the
wheat is dry put into a large bowl
with all the remaining ingredients
and toss together carefully so that
the cheese does not break up. Allow
the salad to chill for up to 1 hour
before serving. If desired, garnish the
salad with whole sprigs of herbs.

Spinach Salad with Bacon, Hazelnuts and Mushrooms

PREPARATION TIME: 20 minutes

COOKING TIME: 2-3 minutes

SERVES: 4 people

675g/1½ lbs spinach, stalks removed,
washed and dried
6 strips bacon/smoked streaky bacon,
bones and rind removed
225g/8oz mushrooms, sliced
120g/4oz/1 cup hazelnuts, roasted,
skinned and roughly chopped

DRESSING
140ml/¼ pint/½ cup oil
45ml/3 tbsps white wine vinegar
5ml/1 tsp Dijon mustard
1 shallot, finely chopped
Salt and pepper
Pinch sugar (optional)

Tear the spinach leaves into bite-size
pieces and put into a serving bowl.
Fry or grill/broil the bacon until
brown and crisp. Crumble the bacon
and sprinkle over the spinach. Add
the hazelnuts and mushrooms to the
spinach salad and toss. Mix all the
dressing ingredients very well and
pour over the salad just before
serving.

Cucumber and Mint Salad

PREPARATION TIME: 30 minutes

SERVES: 4 people

1 large or 2 small cucumbers, peeled for a
striped effect or scratched with the

prongs of a fork lengthwise along the
skin
Salt

DRESSING
280ml/½ pint/1 cup sour cream or
natural yogurt
30ml/2 tbsps chopped fresh mint
15ml/1 tbsp chopped parsley
Pinch sugar
Squeeze lemon juice
Salt and pepper

GARNISH
Whole sprigs of mint

Slice the cucumber thinly in rounds.
Place the cucumber in a colander and
sprinkle lightly with salt. Leave for
30 minutes to drain. Rinse the
cucumber under cold water to
remove the salt and pat dry. Mix the
sour cream or yogurt with the sugar,
lemon juice, salt, pepper, mint and
parsley. Pour over the drained
cucumber and toss. Leave
refrigerated for 30 minutes before
serving, and garnish with whole
sprigs of mint.

Potato Salad with Mustard-Chive Dressing

PREPARATION TIME: 25 minutes

COOKING TIME: 20 minutes

SERVES: 6 people

1.5kg/3lbs potatoes, new or red variety
6 sticks celery, thinly sliced
1 red pepper, seeded, cored and diced
3 hard-boiled eggs

DRESSING
280ml/½ pint/1 cup prepared
mayonnaise
280ml/½ pint/1 cup natural yogurt
60ml/4 tbsp Dijon mustard and mild
mustard mixed half and half
1 bunch chives, snipped
Salt and pepper

Facing page: Cucumber and Mint
Salad (top), and Cracked Wheat
Salad (bottom).

Cook the potatoes in their skins for about 20 minutes in salted water. When the potatoes are tender, drain and peel while still warm. Cut the potatoes into cubes and mix with the celery and red pepper. Set the potato salad aside to cool while mixing the dressing. Combine the mayonnaise, yogurt, mustard, half the chives, salt and pepper and mix well. Toss carefully with the potato salad so that the potatoes do not break up. Spoon the salad into a serving dish and slice the hard-boiled eggs into rounds, or chop roughly. Arrange the hard-boiled eggs in circles on top of the potato salad or scatter over, if chopped. Sprinkle over reserved chives and refrigerate for about 1 hour before serving.

Red, Green and Yellow Pepper Salad

PREPARATION TIME: 20 minutes

SERVES: 6 people

3 sweet red peppers
3 green peppers
3 yellow peppers
Oil
60g/2oz/½ cup small black olives, stoned
30ml/2 tbsps finely chopped coriander leaves
3 hard-boiled eggs

DRESSING
90ml/6 tbsps oil
10ml/2 tsps lemon juice
30ml/2 tbsps white wine vinegar
1 small clove garlic, finely minced
Pinch salt
Pinch cayenne pepper
Pinch sugar (optional)

Cut all the peppers in half and remove the seeds and cores. Press lightly with palm to flatten. Brush the skin side of each pepper with oil and place under a preheated grill/broiler about 15cm/6 inches from the heat. Cook until the skin chars. Remove and wrap the peppers in a clean towel. Leave them to cool 10-15 minutes. Mix the dressing ingredients and quarter the eggs. Unwrap the peppers and peel off the skin. Cut the peppers into strips about 2.5cm/

1 inch wide and arrange in a circle, alternating colours. Arrange the olives and quartered egg in the centre. Sprinkle the coriander leaves over the peppers and spoon over the dressing. Leave the salad, covered, in the refrigerator for 1 hour before serving. Peeled peppers will keep covered in oil up to 5 days in the refrigerator.

Coleslaw

PREPARATION TIME: 25 minutes

SERVES: 6 people

DRESSING
280ml/½ pint/1 cup prepared mayonnaise
4 spring/green onions finely chopped
280ml/½ pint/1 cup sour cream
60g/2oz Roquefort or blue cheese

This page: Zanzibar Prawns/ Shrimp. Facing page: Coleslaw (top), and Potato Salad with Mustard-Chive Dressing (bottom).

1.25ml/¼ tsp Worcestershire sauce
5ml/1 tsp vinegar
30ml/2 tbsps chopped parsley
Pinch sugar
Salt and pepper

SALAD
1 medium size head white cabbage, shredded
6 carrots, peeled and coarsely grated
1 green pepper, cut into thin short strips
120g/4oz/1 cup roasted peanuts or raisins

Combine all the dressing ingredients, reserving half the parsley, and refrigerate in a covered bowl for about 1 hour to allow the flavours to blend. Combine the dressing with the salad ingredients and toss to serve. Sprinkle on reserved chopped parsley.

Zanzibar Prawns/Shrimp

PREPARATION TIME: 25 minutes

COOKING TIME: 18-23 minutes

SERVES: 4 people

450g/1lb king prawns/jumbo shrimp,
  shelled and de-veined
1 large fresh pineapple, peeled, cored and
  cut into chunks
Oil

SAUCE
140ml/¼ pint/½ cup orange juice
15ml/1 tbsp vinegar
15ml/1 tbsp lime juice
5ml/1 tsp dry mustard
15ml/1 tbsp brown sugar
Remaining pineapple

GARNISH
Flaked coconut
Curly endive

Thread the prawns/shrimp and pineapple pieces on skewers, alternating each ingredient. Use about 4 pineapple pieces per skewer. Place the remaining pineapple and the sauce ingredients into a food processor and purée. Pour into a small pan and cook over low heat for about 10-15 minutes to reduce slightly. Place the kebabs on a lightly oiled rack above the coals and cook about 6 minutes, basting frequently with the sauce. Sprinkle cooked kebabs with coconut and serve on endive leaves. Serve remaining sauce separately.

Egg Mayonnaise with Asparagus and Caviar

PREPARATION TIME: 25 minutes

COOKING TIME: 10 minutes

SERVES: 4-6 people

12 asparagus spears, trimmed and peeled
6 hard-boiled eggs
430ml/¾ pint/1½ cups prepared
  mayonnaise
15ml/1 tbsp lemon juice
Hot water
Red caviar

Tie asparagus in a bundle and cook in a deep saucepan of boiling salted water, keeping the asparagus tips out of the water. The tips will cook in the steam and the thick stalks will cook in the water, thus helping the asparagus to cook evenly. Cook about 5-8 minutes or until just tender. Rinse under cold water and

This page: Red, Green and Yellow Pepper Salad. Facing page: Avocado Cream Soup (top) and Tomato and Cucumber Soup (bottom).

drain. Meanwhile, place eggs in boiling water. Bring water back to the boil and cook eggs for 10 minutes. Cool completely under cold running water and peel. Combine mayonnaise and lemon juice. If very thick, add enough hot water until of coating consistency. Arrange eggs cut side down on a plate and coat with the mayonnaise. Surround with asparagus and garnish the eggs with caviar.

COLD SOUPS

Tomato and Cucumber Soup

PREPARATION TIME:
20 minutes, plus chilling time

SERVES: 4 people

6 tomatoes, skinned
2 large cucumbers, peeled and cut
    into pieces, reserving 5cm (2") at
    end for garnish
45ml (3 tbsps) lemon juice
150ml (¼ pint) soured cream
1 onion, peeled and grated
1 tsp tomato purée
Salt
Pepper

Garnish
Cucumber slices

Chop tomatoes. Remove pips.
Strain juice, and discard pips. Put
tomato flesh and juice, cucumber,
onion, tomato purée and lemon
juice into a blender. Blend at high
speed for a few minutes until
smooth. Stir in soured cream, and
salt and pepper to taste. Serve
chilled, garnished with cucumber
slices.

Prawn and Cucumber Soup

PREPARATION TIME:
20 minutes, plus chilling time

SERVES: 4 people

450g (1lb) prawns, cooked, shelled
    and de-veined
200g (7oz) cream cheese
1 small cucumber
½ tsp dry mustard
Salt
White pepper
150ml (¼ pint) single cream
300ml (½ pint) milk

Garnish
Finely sliced cucumber
Dill

Finely chop prawns. Peel and slice
cucumber. Place prawns, cucumber,
mustard, white pepper and a pinch
of salt in a bowl. Beat cream cheese
until soft and creamy, and gradually
add cream and milk. Add cucumber
and prawn mixture, and blend
thoroughly. Cover and chill. If

Avocado Cream Soup

PREPARATION TIME:
10 minutes, plus chilling time

SERVES: 4 people

1¼ cups good, fat-free chicken stock
2 ripe avocados
1 tbsp lemon juice
⅔ cup milk
⅔ cup light cream
Salt and white pepper

Garnish
Snipped chives, if desired

Peel avocados, remove seeds, chop
and put in blender with cream,
lemon juice and milk, and blend
until smooth. Put avocado mixture
and chicken stock in a bowl, and
stir until combined. Push through a
strainer. Season with salt and white
pepper. Chill in refrigerator.
Garnish with chives, if desired.

Raspberry Soup

PREPARATION TIME:
5 minutes, plus chilling time

COOKING TIME: 20 minutes

SERVES: 4 people

1 cup raspberries, fresh, or frozen and
    thawed
2 tbsps lemon juice
3 tbsps sweet sherry
2 tbsps sugar
1¼ cups light cream
1¼ cups water
Crushed ice

Put sugar, raspberries, lemon juice,
sherry and water in a pan, and heat
gently for 10 minutes. Bring to the
boil and simmer for 5 minutes.
Remove from heat and push
through a strainer, and allow to
cool. Stir in cream. Chill. Serve
with crushed ice.

necessary, thin soup further with
milk. Garnish with sliced cucumber
and dill.

Blackberry and Apple Soup

PREPARATION TIME:
5 minutes, plus chilling time

COOKING TIME: 30 minutes

SERVES: 4 people

2 cups blackberries, fresh, or frozen
    and thawed
2 apples, peeled, cored and sliced
¼ cup sugar
2½ cups water
Crushed ice

Place apples and water in a pan and
bring to the boil. Simmer covered
for 15 minutes until apples are
softened. Add sugar and blackberries, and simmer a further
15 minutes. Purée and push
through a strainer. Chill. Serve with
crushed ice.

Rhubarb Soup

PREPARATION TIME:
15 minutes, plus chilling time

COOKING TIME: 20 minutes

SERVES: 4 people

2 cups rhubarb, trimmed and cut into
    1" lengths

2 tbsps redcurrant jelly
¼ cup sugar
1¼ cups orange juice
1¼ cups water

Garnish
Slivered, pared rind of orange

Place rhubarb, redcurrant jelly,
sugar and water in pan. Cover and
heat gently for 10 minutes. Add
orange juice and bring to the boil.
Simmer uncovered for 5 minutes.
Remove from heat, and allow to
cool. Purée or push through a
strainer, and chill. Serve garnished
with slivered orange rind and
crushed ice if desired.

Blackberry and Apple
Soup (left), Rhubarb
Soup (centre), Raspberry
Soup (bottom) and
Prawn and Cucumber
Soup (facing page).

Vichyssoise (Leek and Potato Soup)

PREPARATION TIME:
15 minutes, plus chilling time

COOKING TIME: 30 minutes

SERVES: 4 people

3 large leeks
2 medium potatoes, peeled and sliced
    thinly
1 small onion, peeled and sliced
30g (1oz) butter or margarine
600ml (1 pint) boiling water
½ chicken stock cube
150ml (¼ pint) single cream
Salt
White pepper

Garnish
Parsley or chives

Wash and trim leeks, discarding roots and any green part. Slice thinly. Melt butter in pan and add leek and onion. Cover, and allow to sweat gently over low heat for about 10 minutes. Dissolve ½ chicken stock cube in boiling water. Add potatoes to leek and pour over the stock. Season to taste. Cover and cook for a further 15 minutes, or until potatoes are soft. Push through a fine sieve. Cool. Stir in cream. Adjust seasoning. Chill well for at least 2 hours. Serve garnished with parsley or snipped chives.

Gazpacho

PREPARATION TIME:
20 minutes, plus chilling time

SERVES: 4 people

450g (1lb) ripe tomatoes, skinned
    and roughly chopped
1 onion, peeled and diced
1 green pepper, cored, seeds removed,
    and diced
Half a cucumber
2 tbsps stale white breadcrumbs
2 cloves garlic, crushed
30ml (2 tbsps) red wine vinegar
1 large can tomato juice
Salt
Pepper

Accompaniments
*Diced cucumber, onion, tomato and
    green pepper*

Soak breadcrumbs in vinegar. Reserve tomato flesh, and half the onion and half the green pepper for garnish. Blend remaining onion and remaining green pepper with tomato juice, breadcrumbs, vinegar, and garlic, and season to taste.

Push through a sieve. Chill well. Meanwhile, skin and chop cucumber. Serve with crushed ice and small bowls of cucumber, onion, tomato and green pepper.

Beetroot Soup

PREPARATION TIME:
10 minutes, plus chilling time

COOKING TIME: 1 hour 15 minutes

SERVES: 4 people

450g (1lb) raw beetroot
1 shallot, peeled and quartered
2 tbsps sugar
15ml (1 tbsp) lemon juice
Bouquet garni
1 litre (2 pints) water
1 chicken stock cube
Salt
Pepper

Bring water to boil. Peel and dice beetroot. Add to water with crumbled stock cube, shallot, bouquet garni, sugar, lemon juice

and salt and pepper. Bring to the boil. Reduce heat, and simmer, uncovered, for about an hour. Blend and push through sieve and leave to cool. When cool, put into refrigerator to chill.

Beetroot Soup (left) and Vichyssoise (Leek and Potato Soup) (bottom).

DIPS AND PATÉS

Tzatziki (Cucumber and Yogurt Salad)

PREPARATION TIME: 15 minutes
SERVES: 4 people

1 cucumber, peeled
1 clove garlic, crushed
1 medium-sized carton plain yogurt
10ml (2 tsps) lemon juice
1 tsp chopped mint
Salt

Garnish
Cucumber slices
Sprig of mint

Grate the cucumber and drain off any excess liquid. Mix cucumber with garlic and yogurt. Stir in lemon juice and mint, and add salt to taste. Garnish with a few cucumber slices and a sprig of mint.

Taramasalata (Cod Roe Salad)

PREPARATION TIME: 30 minutes
SERVES: 4 people

225g (8oz) smoked cod roe
½ onion, peeled and grated
2 cloves garlic, crushed
115g (4oz) white bread, crusts
    removed
60ml (4 tbsps) milk
90ml (6 tbsps) olive oil
30ml (2 tbsps) lemon juice
Pepper

Garnish
Lemon
Parsley

Crumble bread into a bowl, and add milk. Leave to soak. Scoop the cod roe out of its skin and break it down with a wooden spoon. Squeeze bread dry in a sieve. Add onion, garlic and bread to cod roe,

This page: Taramasalata (Cod Roe Salad) (top) and Tzatziki (Cucumber and Yogurt Salad) (bottom).

Facing page: Gazpacho

and mix well. Very gradually add oil and lemon juice, alternating between the two. Beat until smooth and creamy. Add pepper to taste, and salt if necessary. Garnish with lemon and parsley, and serve with Melba toast (see recipe for Guacamole) or sliced French loaf, and unsalted butter.

Crudités with Anchovy Dip, Oxford Dip, and Tomato and Chilli Dip

Crudités
Half a cauliflower, broken into florets
Half a cucumber, cut into batons
115g (4oz) button mushrooms, cleaned
3 carrots, scraped and cut into sticks
8 small radishes, cleaned
1 red pepper, cored, seeds removed, and cut into strips
8 spring onions, trimmed
2 courgettes, cut into strips

Anchovy Dip
45g (1½ oz) can anchovy fillets, drained and mashed
2 cloves garlic, crushed
30g (1oz) butter or margarine
150ml (¼ pint) double cream, lightly whipped
1 tsp marjoram or oregano
1 tsp chopped fresh parsley
Pinch sugar or salt, to taste

Melt butter in pan, add garlic, and cook for 1 minute. Add anchovies, herbs and sugar or salt to taste. Cook for 10 minutes, stirring continuously. Set aside. When cool, fold in whipped cream. Chill.

Oxford Dip
Pared rind of 1 lemon
5ml (1 tsp) lemon juice
1 tsp English mustard
½ tsp grated root ginger
2 tbsps redcurrant jelly
60ml (4 tbsps) red wine
1 tsp arrowroot

Blanch rind in boiling water for 30 seconds. Remove and shred finely. Put all ingredients except wine and arrowroot into a pan, and bring to the boil, stirring continuously. When mixed, stir in wine and simmer, uncovered, for 15 minutes. Slake arrowroot in 15ml (1 tbsp) of water and add to pan. Simmer a further 3 minutes, stirring continuously. Chill.

Tomato and Chilli Dip
400g (14oz) can plum tomatoes, drained, reserving juice, and pips removed
1 red chilli, seeds removed, sliced finely
1 clove garlic
1 onion, peeled and chopped finely
15ml (1 tbsp) lemon juice or white wine vinegar
1 tbsp chopped fresh parsley
15g (½ oz) butter or margarine
Salt
Pepper

Melt butter in pan. Add garlic and fry until browned. Discard garlic. Add onion and cook gently till softened. Add chilli and cook a further 3 minutes. Add tomatoes, lemon juice or vinegar, reserved tomato juice and salt and pepper and simmer gently for 10 minutes. Remove from heat and set aside to cool. Push through a sieve, stir in parsley, and chill.

Pâté aux Herbes

PREPARATION TIME:	20 minutes
COOKING TIME:	1 hour
OVEN TEMPERATURE: 170°C; 350°F; Gas Mark 2	
SERVES:	4 people

450g (1lb) pork, finely minced
325g (11oz) packet frozen spinach
225g (8oz) rashers of streaky bacon, rind removed
1 onion, peeled and chopped
2 cloves garlic, crushed
2 tbsps finely chopped fresh basil
2 tbsps chopped parsley
Freshly grated nutmeg
Freshly ground black pepper
½ tsp sage
1 can leg or shoulder ham
1 egg, lightly beaten
Pinch of cayenne pepper
150ml (¼ pint) double cream
Salt

Cook spinach in boiling salted water for 5 minutes. Drain and press between two plates to remove excess water. Chop finely and mix with pork. Combine onion, garlic, herbs and spices, cayenne pepper, cream, and salt and pepper. Cut ham into strips. Line bottom and sides of ovenproof tureen with rashers of streaky bacon. Mix pork and spinach into cream mixture. Add egg and stir thoroughly. Press one-third mixture into tureen. Add half the ham strips. Repeat until all ham and mixture is used up. Cook in a slow oven for 45 minutes. Remove from oven, cool, and serve sliced.

Guacamole

PREPARATION TIME:	15 minutes
COOKING TIME:	5 minutes
SERVES:	4 people

2 ripe avocados
15ml (1 tbsp) lemon juice
1 clove garlic, crushed
1 red chilli, seeds removed, sliced finely
1 shallot, very finely chopped, or grated
¼ tsp ground chilli powder
Pinch of paprika
Salt

Garnish
Lemon slices and parsley
Serve with melba toast if desired

Blanch chilli and shallot in boiling water for 2 minutes. Drain and set aside. Peel the avocados. Pierce the skin with the point of a sharp knife and run down from top to bottom of the pear in quarters. Pull skin back off fruit and remove stone from centre and any dark bits of flesh. Mash the flesh to a purée and mix in lemon juice. Stir in garlic and shallot. Add chilli, chilli powder, paprika and salt, a bit at a time, to desired taste. Garnish with lemon and parsley. Serve with Melba toast if desired.

Melba Toast
Pre-heat grill. Put slices of bread in toaster and toast until golden brown. Remove crusts and cut horizontally through toast whilst still hot. Cut into triangles and toast untoasted side under the grill until golden brown. Keep inside a clean tea-towel until ready to serve.

Crudités (right) with Anchovy Dip (bottom), Oxford Dip (far right) and Tomato and Chilli Dip (below).

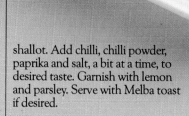

Tomato, Carrot and Spinach Slice

PREPARATION TIME:
30 minutes, plus chilling time

SERVES: 4 people

6 tomatoes, skinned, with pips removed
450g (1lb) spinach, cooked
Pinch of nutmeg
3 carrots, finely grated
150ml (¼ pint) double cream, whipped
11g (⅓ oz) gelatine
60ml (4 tbsps) water
Salt
Pepper

Grease and line a loaf tin with greaseproof paper. Blend tomato in a food processor until smooth. Add salt and pepper to taste. Set aside. Put water in a small bowl. Sprinkle over gelatine and leave 15 minutes to soak. Place bowl in a saucepan of hot water, so that water is part way up side of bowl. Heat gently until gelatine has dissolved. Meanwhile, chop spinach, squeeze out excess liquid and stir in half the cream. Add nutmeg, and salt and pepper to taste. Set aside. Stir one-third of gelatine into tomato mixture, and return bowl of gelatine to saucepan. Fill tomato into loaf tin. Level out, and put into freezer compartment. Leave 10 minutes. Meanwhile, stir carrot and remaining cream together. Stir half of remaining gelatine into carrot mixture, and pour over tomato mixture. Return tin to freezer for 10 minutes. Stir remaining gelatine into spinach mixture, and pour onto carrot layer. Smooth out and put into freezer for a further 10 minutes. Remove from freezer and chill in refrigerator overnight.

This page: Tomato, Carrot and Spinach Slice.

Facing page: Salmon, Watercress and Tomato Slice (top) and Pâté aux Herbes (bottom).

Salmon, Watercress and Tomato Slice

PREPARATION TIME: 30 minutes

SERVES: 4 people

6 tomatoes, skinned, and pips removed
Half a bunch of watercress
225g (8oz) can red or pink salmon
150ml (¼ pint) double cream, whipped
11g (⅓ oz) gelatine
60ml (4 tbsps) water
Salt
Pepper

Garnish
Watercress

Grease and line a loaf tin with greaseproof paper. Drain, and place salmon and one-third of the cream into a food processor, and process until smooth. Add salt and pepper to taste. Set aside. Put water in a small bowl, and sprinkle over gelatine. Leave 15 minutes to soak. Place bowl in a sauepan of hot water so that water is partway up side of bowl. Heat gently until gelatine has dissolved. Meanwhile, chop watercress, squeeze out excess liquid, and stir in half the remaining cream. Add salt and pepper to taste. Set aside. Place tomatoes and remaining cream in food processor, and process. Stir one-third of gelatine into tomato mixture and return bowl of gelatine to saucepan. Fill tomato into loaf tin. Level out, and put into freezer compartment for 10 minutes. Stir half the remaining gelatine into watercress mixture and pour over tomato mixture. Return tin to freezer for 10 minutes. Stir remaining gelatine into salmon mixture and pour onto watercress layer. Smooth out and put into freezer for 10 minutes. Remove from freezer and chill in refrigerator overnight. Garnish with watercress.

Salmon Pâté

PREPARATION TIME: 15 minutes

SERVES: 4 people

225g (8oz) can red or pink salmon, drained
115g (4oz) curd cheese
30g (1oz) butter
Pinch of ground mace or ground nutmeg
Few drops of lemon juice
¼ tsp tabasco sauce
30ml (2 tbsps) double cream
Salt
Pepper

Garnish
Gherkins (slice each gherkin horizontally 4 or 5 times, and splay into a fan)

Remove any bones from salmon. Work into a paste with the back of a spoon. Cream the butter and cheese until smooth. Add salmon, lemon juice, seasonings and cream, and mix well. Put into a large dish or individual ramekins. Garnish dish with a gherkin fan.

Chicken Liver Pâté

PREPARATION TIME: 15 minutes

COOKING TIME: 15 minutes

SERVES: 4 people

225g (8oz) chicken livers, trimmed
1 onion, peeled and diced finely
30g (1oz) butter for frying
60g (2oz) butter, creamed
1 clove garlic, crushed
15ml (1 tbsp) brandy
5ml (1 tsp) Worcestershire sauce
Salt
Pepper

Garnish
Dill

Heat butter in frying pan. Add garlic, onions, salt, and freshly ground black pepper, and fry gently until onions have softened. Increase heat, and sauté chicken livers in hot butter for about 2 minutes on each side, until just cooked through. Add Worcestershire sauce and stir. Blend contents of frying pan and push through a wire sieve with the back of a spoon into a bowl. Beat in creamed butter, brandy, and adjust seasoning. Place in one large dish or individual ramekin dishes. If not being eaten straight away, seal surface with clarified butter and refrigerate. Garnish with dill.

Smoked Mackerel Pâté

PREPARATION TIME: 30 minutes, plus chilling time

SERVES: 4 people

225g (8oz) smoked mackerel fillets, skinned and bones removed
60g (2oz) butter
Juice of half an orange
1 tsp tomato purée
5ml (1 tsp) white wine vinegar
Black pepper, freshly ground
Salt, if desired

Garnish
1 can pimentos

Aspic
300ml (½ pint) clear, strained chicken stock
2 tsps powdered gelatine
30ml (2 tbsps) dry sherry
30ml (2 tbsps) cold water
or
1 packet commercial aspic, used as directed

Cream butter. Place butter, smoked mackerel, orange juice, tomato purée, vinegar and black pepper in a blender. Blend until smooth. Add salt if necessary. Place in one dish or individual dishes. Cut pimentos into strips. Sprinkle gelatine over a small bowl with 15-30ml (1-2 tbsps) of cold water in it and leave to soak for 15 minutes. Place bowl in a saucepan of simmering water, and leave until gelatine has dissolved. Heat stock in pan. Add gelatine. Allow to cool, and stir in sherry. Make a lattice of pimento on top of mackerel pâté. Carefully pour over aspic to just cover pimento. Chill in refrigerator.

Smoked Mackerel Pâté (right) and Salmon Pâté (bottom).

BARBECUED MEAT AND POULTRY

Kashmiri Lamb Kebabs

PREPARATION TIME: 20 minutes

COOKING TIME: 10 minutes

SERVES: 4 people

675g/1½ lbs lamb shoulder or leg
30ml/2 tbsps oil
1 clove garlic, finely minced
15ml/1 tbsp ground cumin
5ml/1 tsp turmeric
5ml/1 tsp grated gresh ginger
Chopped fresh coriander or parsley leaves
Salt and pepper
1 red pepper, cut in 2.5cm/1 inch pieces
1 small onion, cut in rings

Cut the lamb in 2.5cm/1 inch cubes. Heat the oil and cook the garlic, cumin, turmeric and ginger for 1 minute. Add the coriander, salt and pepper. Allow to cool and then rub the spice mixture over the meat. Leave covered in the refrigerator for several hours. Thread the meat on skewers, alternating with the pepper slices. Cook about 10 minutes, turning frequently. During the last 5 minutes of cooking, thread sliced onion rings around the meat and continue cooking until the onion is cooked and slightly browned and meat has reached desired doneness.

Minced Lamb Kebabs with Olives and Tomatoes

PREPARATION TIME: 20 minutes

COOKING TIME: 10 minutes

SERVES: 4 people

30g/1oz/4 tbsps bulgur wheat, soaked and drained

550g/1¼lbs minced/ground lamb
1 clove garlic, finely minced
10ml/2 tsps ground cumin
Pinch cinnamon
Salt and pepper
1 egg, beaten
Oil
16 large green olives, stoned
16 cherry tomatoes

This page: Mustard Grilled Pork with Poppy Seeds. Facing page: Kashmiri Lamb Kebabs (left) and Minced Lamb Kebabs with Olives and Tomatoes (right).

SAUCE
280ml/½ pint/1 cup yogurt
30ml/2 tbsps chopped fresh mint
Salt and pepper

Soak the bulgur wheat until soft. Wring out and spread on paper towels to drain and dry. Mix with the remaining ingredients and enough of the beaten egg to bind together. The mixture should not be too wet. Form into small balls about 3.75cm/ 1½ inches in diameter. Thread onto skewers with the olives and tomatoes. Brush with oil and grill about 10 minutes, turning frequently. Mix the yogurt, mint, salt and pepper and serve with the kebabs.

Mustard Grilled Pork with Poppy Seeds

PREPARATION TIME: 20 minutes plus marinating time

COOKING TIME: 45 minutes to 1 hour

SERVES: 4-6 people

4 175-200g/6-7oz whole pork fillets/ tenderloin
30ml/2 tbsps black poppy seeds

MARINADE
15ml/1 tbsp mild mustard
60ml/4 tbsps oil
60ml/4 tbsps unsweetened apple juice
1 clove garlic, finely minced
Salt and pepper

SWEET MUSTARD SAUCE
280ml/½ pint/1 cup mild mustard
60g/2oz/¼ cup brown sugar
60ml/2 fl oz/¼ cup dry cider or unsweetened apple juice
10ml/2 tsps chopped fresh or crumbled dried tarragon
Pinch cayenne pepper
Salt

Mix the marinade and rub into the pork. Place the pork in a dish or pan and cover. Refrigerate for 4 hours or overnight. Using a grill with an adjustable rack, place the pork over the coals on the highest level or set an electric or gas grill to a medium temperature. Cook the pork for 45

minutes-1 hour, basting with the marinade and turning frequently. Lower the shelf or raise the temperature. Baste frequently with the sauce during the last 10 minutes of cooking time. During the last 5 minutes, sprinkle the pork fillets with the poppy seeds. Serve the pork sliced thinly with the remaining sauce.

Turkey and Pancetta Rolls

PREPARATION TIME: 30 minutes

COOKING TIME: 20-30 minutes

SERVES: 4-6 people

2 turkey breasts, 450g/1lb each, skinned
90g/3oz/⅓ cup butter softened
1 clove garlic, minced
15ml/1 tbsp oregano leaves
16 slices pancetta or prosciutto ham
Salt and pepper
Oil

Cut the turkey breasts in half, lengthwise. Place each piece between two sheets of clingfilm/plastic wrap and bat out each piece with a rolling pin or meat mallet to flatten. Mix the butter, garlic, oregano, salt and pepper together. Spread half of the mixture over each slice of turkey. Lay 4 slices of pancetta on top of each piece of turkey. Roll up, tucking in the sides and tie with fine string in 3 places. Spread the remaining butter on the outside of each roll. Cook the rolls over medium hot coals until tender. Insert a meat thermometer into each roll to check doneness. The temperature should read 90°C/ 190°F. Cooking should take approximately 20 to 30 minutes. Slice each roll into 1.25cm/½ inch rounds to serve.

Niçoise Chicken

PREPARATION TIME: 30 minutes

COOKING TIME: 20 minutes

SERVES: 4 people

4 boned chicken breasts, unskinned
60ml/4 tbsps oil
30ml/2 tbsps lemon juice

TAPENADE FILLING
450g/1lb large black olives, stoned
60ml/2 tbsps capers
1 clove garlic, peeled and roughly chopped
4 anchovy fillets
30ml/2 tbsps olive oil
Raw tomato sauce

450g/1lb ripe tomatoes, peeled, seeded and chopped
1 shallot, very finely chopped
30ml/2 tbsps chopped parsley
30ml/2 tbsps chopped basil
30ml/2 tbsps white wine vinegar
30ml/2 tbsps olive oil
15ml/1 tbsp sugar
Salt and pepper
15ml/1 tbsp tomato purée/paste (optional)

Cut a pocket in the thickest side of the chicken breasts. Combine half the olives, half the capers and the remaining ingredients for the tapenade in a blender or food processor. Work to a purée. Add the remaining olives and capers and process a few times to chop them roughly. Fill the chicken breasts with the tapenade. Chill to help filling to firm. Baste the skin side with oil and lemon juice mixed together. Cook skin side down first for 10 minutes over medium hot coals. Turn over, baste again and grill for another 10 minutes on the other side. Meanwhile, combine the sauce ingredients and mix very well. Serve with the chicken.

Orange Grilled Duck with Sesame and Spice

PREPARATION TIME: 20 minutes, plus marinating time

COOKING TIME: 40 minutes

SERVES: 4 people

4 boned duck breasts
60ml/4 tbsps sesame seeds

Facing page: Turkey and Pancetta Rolls (top) and Niçoise Chicken (bottom).

minutes before the duck is cooked, sprinkle the orange slices with brown sugar and grill on both sides to glaze. Serve with the duck.

Herb and Onion Grilled Lamb Chops

PREPARATION TIME: 10 minutes

COOKING TIME: 15 minutes

SERVES: 4 people

4 leg chops, cut 2cm/¾ inch thick

MARINADE
1 large onion, finely chopped
15ml/1 tbsp parsley, finely chopped
15ml/1 tbsp fresh thyme or mint leaves, roughly chopped
2 fresh bay leaves, cut in thin shreds with scissors
1 clove garlic, finely minced
45ml/3 tbsps oil
Juice of ½ lemon
Salt and pepper

Combine all the marinade ingredients and pour over the chops in a dish. Leave, covered, 2 hours in the refrigerator. Place on a rack over hot coals and cook the chops 15 minutes, turning often and basting frequently with the remaining marinade.

Barbecued Flank Steak

PREPARATION TIME: 25 minutes

COOKING TIME: 45-55 minutes

SERVES: 6 people

1.5kg/3½ lbs skirt steak/flank steak, in one piece

BARBECUE SEASONING
60ml/4 tbsps salt
7.5ml/1½ tsp freshly ground pepper
7.5ml/1½ tsp cayenne pepper (or paprika for a milder tasting mixture)

MARINADE
60ml/4 tbsps soy sauce
120ml/4 fl oz/½ cup dry white wine
45ml/3 tbsps oil
Pinch ground nutmeg
Pinch ground ginger
Pinch ground mustard
Salt and pepper

SAUCE
Reserved marinade
180ml/6 fl oz/¾ cup orange juice
1 shallot, finely chopped
10ml/2 tsps cornflour/cornstarch

GARNISH
1 orange, peeled and thinly sliced in rounds
Brown sugar

Score the fat side of each duck breast with a sharp knife. Mix the marinade ingredients together and pour over the duck in a shallow dish. Cover and refrigerate for 2 hours. Turn the duck frequently. Place the duck breasts fat side down on grill. Cook for 20 minutes per side, basting frequently. If the duck appears to be cooking too quickly, turn more often. Combine the sauce ingredients and add any remaining marinade. Cook 1 to 2 minutes over moderate heat until boiling and, just before the duck is finished cooking, brush the fat side lightly with the sauce and sprinkle on the sesame seeds. Turn fat side down onto the grill for 1 minute. Serve remaining sauce with the duck. Five

This page: Orange Grilled Duck with Sesame and Spice. **Facing page:** Herb and Onion Grilled Lamb Chops (top), and Barbecued Flank Steak (bottom).

Barbecued Ribs

PREPARATION TIME: 15 minutes

COOKING TIME: 2 hours

SERVES: 4-6 people

2-3 racks pork spare ribs (about 2.5kg/ 5lbs)
Barbecue Sauce (see recipe for Barbecued Flank Steak)
or
Sweet Mustard Sauce (see recipe for Mustard Grilled Pork with Poppy Seeds)

Leave the ribs in whole racks. Combine the ingredients for either sauce and pour over the meat in a roasting pan. Cover with foil and bake, turning and basting frequently, for 1 hour in a 150°C/325°F/ Gas Mark 3 oven. Uncover and bake 30 minutes more in the oven. Finish on a barbecue grill over moderately hot coals for about 30 minutes, basting frequently with the sauce. Cut between the bones into pieces. Serve with the remaining sauce.

Javanese Pork

PREPARATION TIME: 20 minutes

COOKING TIME: 30-45 minutes

SERVES: 4 people

4 pork rib or loin chops cut 2.5cm/1 inch thick
60ml/4 tbsps dark soy sauce
Large pinch cayenne pepper
45ml/3 tbsps lime or lemon juice
15ml/1 tbsp ground coriander
30ml/2 tbsps oil
30ml/2 tbsps brown sugar
4 medium-sized sweet red peppers
Oil
1 bunch fresh coriander

Snip the fat around the edges of the chops at 1.25cm/½ inch intervals to prevent curling. Mix soy sauce, cayenne pepper, lemon juice, coriander and oil together in a dish or pan. Place the pork chops in the

This page: Javanese Pork. Facing page: Chinese Pork and Aubergine/ Eggplant Kebabs (left), and Barbecued Ribs (right).

BARBECUE SAUCE
60ml/4 tbsps oil
340ml/12 fl oz/1¼ cups tomato ketchup
45ml/3 tbsps Worcestershire sauce
90ml/6 tbsps cider vinegar
60ml/4 tbsps soft brown sugar
60ml/4 tbsps chopped onion
1 clove garlic, crushed (optional)
1 bay leaf
60ml/4 tbsps water
10ml/2 tsps dry mustard
Dash tabasco
Salt and pepper

First prepare the barbecue sauce. Combine all the ingredients, reserving salt and pepper to add later. Cook in a heavy saucepan over low heat for 30 minutes, stirring frequently and adding more water if the sauce reduces too quickly.

Remove the bay leaf and add salt and pepper to taste before using. The sauce should be thick. Use the sauce for basting while cooking, or serve hot to accompany cooked meat and poultry. Score the meat across both sides with a large knife. Mix together the barbecue seasoning and rub 30ml/2 tbsps over the meat, reserving the rest of the seasoning for other use. Sear the meat on both sides over hot coals. Raise the grill rack or lower the temperature on a gas or electric grill/broiler. Baste with the sauce and grill the meat slowly. During last 5 minutes, lower the rack or raise the temperature and grill the meat quickly on both sides, basting with the sauce. Slice the meat thinly across the grain and serve with any remaining sauce.

**This page: Stuffed Hamburgers.
Facing page: Butterflied Lamb.**

Alternatively, make shallow cuts halfway through the thickest parts and press open. Thread two or three long skewers through the meat – this will make the meat easier to handle and turn on the grill. Place in a plastic bag or large, shallow dish. Mix the other ingredients together and pour over the lamb, rubbing it in well. Cover the dish or seal the bag and leave at room temperature for 6 hours or overnight in the refrigerator. Turn the lamb frequently. Remove from the dish or the bag and reserve the marinade. Grill at least 15cm/ 6 inches away from the coals on the skin side first. Grill 20 minutes per side for pink lamb and 30-40 minutes per side for more well done lamb. Baste frequently during grilling. Remove the skewers and cut the slices across the grain. If fresh mint is unavailable, use rosemary, fresh or dried. Alternatively, roast lamb in a 180°C/350°F/Gas Mark 4 oven for half of the cooking time and grill for the last half of cooking.

Stuffed Hamburgers

| **PREPARATION TIME:** 30 minutes |
| **COOKING TIME:** 20 minutes |
| **SERVES:** 4-8 people |

900g/2lbs minced/ground beef
1 onion, finely chopped
60ml/4 tbsps Worcestershire sauce
Salt and pepper
8 hamburger buns

GUACAMOLE BURGERS

FILLING
120g/4oz Tilsit or Monterey Jack cheese, cubed
1 mild chili pepper, thinly sliced and seeds removed

TOPPING
1 avocado, peeled and mashed
1 small clove garlic, crushed
10ml/2 tsps lemon or lime juice
1 tomato, peeled, seeded and finely chopped
Salt and pepper

BLUE CHEESE BURGERS
FILLING
120g/4oz blue cheese, crumbled
30g/1oz/¼ cup chopped walnuts

marinade and leave, covered, in the refrigerator for 1 hour. Turn over after 30 minutes. Place on grill over medium hot coals or on a middle rack. Mix sugar into remaining marinade. Cook chops for 15-20 minutes on each side until well done. Baste with the marinade frequently during the last 10-15 minutes of cooking. Meanwhile, wash and dry the peppers and brush with oil on all sides. Place alongside pork for half of its cooking time. Turn the peppers often. They will soften and char on the outside. Serve the pork chops with peppers and garnish with coriander leaves.

Butterflied Lamb

| **PREPARATION TIME:** 30 minutes, plus marinating time |
| **COOKING TIME:** 40-50 minutes |
| **SERVES:** 6-8 people |

1.8kg/4lbs leg of lamb
75ml/5 tbsps oil
Juice and rind of one lemon
Small bunch mint, roughly chopped
Salt and coarsely ground black pepper
1 clove garlic, crushed

To butterfly the lamb, cut through the skin along the line of the main bone down to the bone. Cut the meat away from the bone, opening out the leg while scraping against the bone with a small, sharp knife. Take out the bone and remove excess fat. Flatten thick places by batting with a rolling pin or meat mallet.

TOPPING
15ml/1 tbsp brown/steak sauce
75ml/5 tbsps prepared mayonnaise
90ml/6 tbsps sour cream or yogurt
Salt and pepper

GRUYÈRE AND MUSHROOM BURGERS
FILLING
60g/2oz mushrooms, roughly chopped
120g/4oz Gruyère or Swiss cheese, cubed

TOPPING
450g/1lb tomatoes
1 clove garlic, finely minced
30ml/2 tbsps tarragon, chopped
15ml/1 tbsp tarragon vinegar
Pinch sugar
30ml/2 tbsps oil
Salt and pepper

Mix the hamburger ingredients well, mould the meat around the chosen fillings and press carefully into patties. Mix the guacamole topping ingredients together and set aside while grilling the hamburgers. Mix the topping for the blue cheese burgers and refrigerate until needed. For the Gruyère burger topping, roughly chop tomatoes and then finely chop in a blender or food processor. Sieve to remove the seeds and skin, combine with the remaining tomato sauce ingredients and mix well. Grill hamburgers over hot coals 10 minutes per side. Quickly grill cut sides of the hamburger buns to heat through and place the hamburgers inside. Spoon on the appropriate toppings for each filling.

Chicken Tikka

PREPARATION TIME: 20 minutes
COOKING TIME: 10-15 minutes
SERVES: 4 people

1.5kg/3lb chicken, skinned and boned

MARINADE
140ml/¼ pint/½ cup natural yogurt
1 small piece ginger, grated
1 clove garlic, finely minced
5ml/1 tsp chili powder, hot or mild
2.5ml/½ tsp ground coriander
2.5ml/½ tsp ground cumin
1.25ml/¼ tsp turmeric

1.25ml/¼ tsp red food colouring (optional)
Juice of one lime
Salt and pepper

Half head Iceberg lettuce, shredded
4 lemon wedges
4 small tomatoes, quartered

Cut chicken into 2.5cm/1 inch pieces. Mix all the marinade ingredients together. Pour over the chicken and stir well. Cover and leave for several hours in the refrigerator. Thread chicken on skewers and grill 10-15 minutes, turning frequently. Baste with any remaining marinade. Serve on a bed of shredded lettuce with tomatoes and lemon wedges.

Indian Chicken

PREPARATION TIME: 15 minutes plus marinating time
COOKING TIME: 45 minutes to 1 hour
SERVES: 4-6 people

1 1.5kg/3lbs chicken, cut into 8 pieces
570ml/1 pint/2 cups natural yogurt
10ml/2 tsps ground coriander
10ml/2 tsps paprika
5ml/1 tsp ground turmeric
Juice of 1 lime
15ml/1 tbsp honey
½ clove garlic, finely minced
1 small piece ginger, peeled and grated

Pierce the chicken all over with a fork or skewer. Combine all the remaining ingredients and spread half the mixture over the chicken, rubbing in well. Place the chicken in a shallow dish or a plastic bag and cover or tie and leave for at last 4 hours or overnight in the refrigerator. If your barbecue has adjustable shelves, place on the level furthest from the coals. Arrange the chicken skin side down and grill until lightly browned, turn over and cook again until lightly browned. Baste frequently with remaining marinade. Lower the grill for the last 15 minutes and cook, turning and basting frequently, until the chicken is brown and the skin is crisp. Alternatively, cook the chicken

in a covered pan in the oven at 150°C/325°F Gas Mark 4 for 45 minutes to 1 hour and grill for the last 15 minutes for flavour and colour. Serve any remaining yogurt mixture separately as a sauce.

Chinese Pork and Aubergine/Eggplant Kebabs

PREPARATION TIME: 20 minutes
COOKING TIME: 15-20 minutes
SERVES: 4 people

450g/1lb pork fillet/tenderloin, cut in 2.5cm/1 inch cubes
2 medium onions, cut in 2.5cm/1 inch pieces
1 large aubergine/eggplant, cut in 3.75cm/1½ inch cubes
30ml/2 tbsps Hoisin sauce
45ml/3 tbsps soy sauce
60ml/4 tbsps rice wine or dry sherry
1 clove garlic, finely minced
Sesame seeds
Salt

Sprinkle the aubergine/eggplant cubes with salt and leave in a colander to drain for 30 minutes. Rinse well and pat dry. Pre-cook in 30ml/2 tbsps oil to soften slightly. Thread the pork, onion and aubergine/eggplant on skewers, alternating the ingredients. Mix the hoisin sauce, soy sauce, rice wine or sherry and garlic together. Brush the kebabs with the mixture and place them on a lightly-oiled grill. Cook about 15-20 minutes, turning and basting frequently. During the last 2 minutes sprinkle all sides with sesame seeds and continue grilling to brown the seeds. Pour over any remaining sauce before serving.

Facing page: Indian Chicken (top), and Chicken Tikka (bottom).

Burgundy Beef Kebabs

PREPARATION TIME: 20 minutes, plus marinating time

COOKING TIME: 10 minutes

SERVES: 4 people

120g/4oz shallots or button onions, parboiled 3 minutes and peeled
670g/1½ lbs sirloin or rump steak, cut in 2.5cm/1 inch thick cubes

MARINADE
280ml/½ pint/1 cup burgundy or other dry red wine
45ml/3 tbsps oil
1 bay leaf
1 clove garlic, peeled
1 sliced onion
6 black peppercorns
1 sprig fresh thyme
Pinch salt

SAUCE
280ml/½ pint/1 cup sour cream
30g/2 tbsps chopped fresh mixed herbs (such as parsley, thyme, marjoram and chervil)
15ml/1 tbsp red wine vinegar
Pinch sugar
10ml/2 tsps Dijon mustard
Salt and pepper

Bring the marinade ingredients to the boil in a small saucepan. Remove from the heat and allow to cool completely. When cold, pour over the meat in a plastic bag. Seal the bag well, but place it in a bowl to catch any drips. Marinate overnight in the refrigerator, turning the bag occasionally. Thread the meat onto skewers with the onions and grill 10 minutes, turning and basting frequently. Mix the sauce ingredients together and serve with the kebabs.

Smoked Sausage and Apple Kebabs

PREPARATION TIME: 20 minutes

COOKING TIME: 6 minutes

SERVES: 4 people

Two rings smoked pork or beef sausage, cut in 2.5cm/1 inch thick slices

4 small apples, quartered and cored
8 sage leaves
Lemon juice
Quarter quantity sweet mustard sauce (see recipe for Mustard Grilled Pork with Poppy Seeds)

Brush the apples with lemon juice. Thread onto skewers, alternating with sausage pieces and bay leaves.

Brush with the mustard sauce and grill 10 minutes, turning frequently and basting with the sauce. Serve any remaining sauce with the kebabs if desired.

Ham and Apricot Kebabs

PREPARATION TIME: 15 minutes

COOKING TIME: 12 minutes

SERVES: 4 people

675g/1½ lbs cooked gammon/ham cut in
   5cm/2 inch cubes
225g/8oz canned or fresh apricots,
   halved and stoned
1 green pepper, cut in 5cm/2 inch pieces

APRICOT BASTE
180g/6oz/¾ cup light brown sugar
60g/4 tbsps apricot jam, sieved
90ml/6 tbsps wine or cider vinegar
5ml/1 tsp dry mustard
45ml/3 tbsps light soy sauce
Salt and pepper

Thread ham, apricots and pepper
pieces onto skewers, alternating the
ingredients. Mix the apricot baste
ingredients together and cook over
gentle heat to dissolve the sugar.
Brush over kebabs as they cook. Turn
and baste several times for about
12 minutes over hot coals. If using
canned apricots, reserve the juice and
add to any baste that remains after
the kebabs are cooked. Bring this
mixture to the boil to reduce slightly
and serve as a sauce with the kebabs.

Spicy Madeira Steaks

PREPARATION TIME: 20 minutes

COOKING TIME: 15 minutes

SERVES: 4 people

4 rump/butt steaks about 180g/6oz each

MARINADE
60ml/4 tbsps oil
140ml/¼ pint/½ cup ketchup
180ml/6 fl oz/¾ cup red wine vinegar
1 clove garlic, crushed
5ml/1 tsp pepper
5ml/1 tsp ground cloves
2.5ml/½ tsp cinnamon
2.5ml/½ tsp thyme leaves

SAUCE
140ml/¼ pint/½ cup reserved marinade
30ml/2 tbsps flour
140ml/¼ pint/½ cup beef stock
140ml/¼ pint/½ cup Madeira
Salt

Combine marinade ingredients and

pour over steaks in a dish. Cover and
refrigerate at least 4 hours. Remove
from marinade and place over hot
coals. Grill, basting frequently, until
of desired doneness. Combine flour
with reserved marinade, beating well
to mix to a smooth paste. Gradually
beat in stock. Bring to the boil in a
small saucepan, stirring constantly.
Cook until thickened, about 1

minute. Reduce heat and simmer 5
minutes. Stir in Madeira and add salt
to taste. Serve with the steak.

**Facing page: Spicy Madeira Steaks
(left), and Burgundy Beef Kebabs
(right). This page: Ham and
Apricot Kebabs (left), and Smoked
Sausage and Apple Kebabs (right).**

BARBECUED FISH AND SEAFOOD

Marsala Fish

PREPARATION TIME: 25 minutes

COOKING TIME: 10-15 minutes

SERVES: 4 people

4 medium sized mackerel, trout or similar
  fish
Juice of 1 lemon
10ml/2 tsps turmeric
2 green chili peppers, finely chopped
1 small piece ginger, grated
1 clove garlic, finely minced
Pinch ground cinnamon
Pinch ground cloves
60ml/4 tbsps oil
Salt and pepper
Fresh coriander leaves

ACCOMPANIMENT
½ cucumber, finely diced
140ml/¼ pint/½ cup thick natural yogurt
1 spring/green onion, finely chopped
Salt and pepper

Clean and gut the fish. Cut three slits on each side of the fish. Combine spices, lemon juice, oil, garlic and chili peppers and spread over the fish and inside the cuts. Place whole sprigs of coriander inside the fish. Brush the grill rack lightly with oil or use a wire fish rack. Cook the fish 10-15 minutes, turning often and basting with any remaining mixture. Combine the accompaniment ingredients and serve with the fish.

Scallops, Bacon and Prawn/Shrimp Kebabs

PREPARATION TIME: 25 minutes

COOKING TIME: 20-25 minutes

SERVES: 4 people

12 large, raw scallops
12 raw king prawns/jumbo shrimp,
  peeled and de-veined
12 slices smoked streaky bacon/bacon
Juice of 1 lemon
60ml/2 tbsps oil
Coarsely ground black pepper

This page: Scallops, Bacon and Prawn/Shrimp Kebabs. Facing page: Marsala Fish.

RED CHILI YOGURT SAUCE
2 cloves garlic, finely chopped
1 red pepper, grilled and peeled
1 red chili pepper, chopped
3 slices bread, crusts removed, soaked in water
45ml/3 tbsps olive oil
140ml/¼ pint/½ cup natural yogurt

Wrap each scallop in a slice of bacon and thread onto skewers, alternating with prawns/shrimp. Mix the lemon juice, oil and pepper and brush over the shellfish as they cook. Turn frequently and cook until the bacon is lightly crisped and the scallops are just firm. Meanwhile, prepare the sauce. Squeeze the bread to remove the water and place the bread in a blender. Add the finely chopped garlic, the chopped red chili pepper and peeled red pepper and blend well. With the machine running, pour in the oil through the funnel in a thin, steady stream. Keep the machine running until the mixture is a smooth, shiny paste. Combine with the yogurt and mix well. Serve with kebabs.

Grilled Sardines with Lemon and Oregano

PREPARATION TIME: 15 minutes

COOKING TIME: 6-8 minutes

SERVES: 4-6 people

8-12 fresh sardines, gutted, scaled, washed and dried
8-12 sprigs fresh oregano
90ml/3 fl oz/⅓ cup olive oil
Juice and rind of 2 lemons
Salt and pepper
15ml/1 tbsp dried oregano

Place one sprig of oregano inside each fish. Mix oil, lemon juice and rind, salt and pepper together. Make two slits on each side of the fish. Brush the fish with the lemon mixture and grill over hot coals for 3-4 minutes per side, basting frequently. When the fish are nearly done, sprinkle the dried oregano on the coals. The smoke will give the fish extra flavour. May be served as a starter/appetizer or main course.

Grey Mullet with Fennel

PREPARATION TIME: 15 minutes

COOKING TIME: 18-22 minutes

SERVES: 4 people

2-4 grey mullet, depending upon size, gutted and cleaned

MARINADE
90ml/3 fl oz/⅓ cup oil
15ml/1 tbsp fennel seeds, slightly crushed
1 clove garlic, finely minced
Juice and rind of one lemon
30ml/2 tbsps chopped fennel tops
Salt and pepper

Heat oil and add the fennel seeds. Cook for one minute. Add the garlic and remaining ingredients except the fennel tops. Leave the mixture to cool completely. Pour over the fish in a shallow dish. Cover and refrigerate for 1 hour. Grill over hot coals 10–12 minutes per side. Sprinkle over fennel tops half way through cooking. Tops may also be placed directly on the coals for aromatic smoke.

Swordfish Steaks with Green Peppercorns and Garlic Oregano Sauce

PREPARATION TIME: 25 minutes

COOKING TIME: 15 minutes

SERVES: 4 people

30ml/2 tbsps fresh green peppercorns (substitute well rinsed canned green peppercorns)
90ml/6 tbsps lemon juice
60ml/4 tbsps olive oil
Salt
4 swordfish steaks (tuna steaks may also be used)

SAUCE
1 egg
1 clove garlic, roughly chopped
140ml/¼ pint/½ cup oil
15ml/1 tbsp lemon juice
2 sprigs fresh oregano
Salt and pepper

Crush the green peppercorns slightly

and mix with lemon juice, oil and salt. Place the swordfish steaks in a shallow dish and pour over the lemon oil mixture. Cover and refrigerate several hours, turning frequently. Process the egg and garlic in a blender or food processor. With the machine running, pour oil through the funnel in a thin, steady stream. When the sauce is thick, strip the leaves off the oregano and process to chop them finely. Add lemon juice, salt and pepper. Grill the swordfish over hot coals for 15 minutes, basting frequently and turning once. Serve with the sauce. (Peppercorns will pop when exposed to the heat of the grill.)

Grilled Red Mullet with Tarragon

PREPARATION TIME: 15 minutes

COOKING TIME: 10-16 minutes

SERVES: 4 people

4 large or 8 small red mullet, gutted, scaled, washed and dried
4 or 8 sprigs fresh tarragon

MARINADE
60ml/4 tbsps oil
30ml/2 tbsps tarragon vinegar
Salt and pepper

SAUCE
1 egg
140ml/¼ pint/½ cup oil
5ml/1 tsp Dijon mustard
15ml/1 tbsp chopped tarragon
15ml/1 tbsp chopped parsley
15ml/1 tbsp tarragon vinegar
30ml/2 tbsps double/heavy cream
5ml/1 tsp brandy
Salt and pepper

Place a sprig of tarragon inside each fish. Cut two slits on the side of each fish. Mix the marinade ingredients together, pour over the fish in a shallow dish and refrigerate for 30 minutes, covered. Put the egg in a

Facing page: Swordfish Steaks with Green Peppercorns and Garlic Oregano Sauce (top), and Grilled Sardines with Lemon and Oregano (bottom).

blender or food processor. Add the mustard, salt and pepper and process to mix. Add the oil through the funnel, with the machine running, in a thin, steady stream. When all the oil has been added, add the herbs, vinegar and brandy and process to mix well. Fold in the double/heavy cream and pour into a serving dish. Keep in the refrigerator until ready to use. Cook the fish for 5 to 8 minutes per side, depending upon size of fish. Baste frequently with the marinade while cooking. Serve with the sauce.

This page: Grey Mullet with Fennel (top), and Grilled Red Mullet with Tarragon (bottom). Facing page: Monkfish and Pepper Kebabs with Bernaise Butter Sauce.

Monkfish and Pepper Kebabs with Bernaise Butter Sauce

PREPARATION TIME: 30 minutes
COOKING TIME: 25 minutes
SERVES: 4 people

450g/1lb monkfish, cut into 5cm/2 inch pieces
8 strips bacon/streaky bacon, rind and bone removed
2 pieces lemon grass
1 green pepper, cut in 5cm/2 inch pieces
1 red pepper, cut in 5cm/2 inch pieces
12 mushroom caps
8 bay leaves
Oil

BERNAISE BUTTER SAUCE
120ml/4 fl oz/½ cup dry white wine
60ml/4 tbsps tarragon vinegar
2 shallots, finely chopped
15ml/1 tbsp chopped fresh tarragon
15ml/1 tbsp chopped fresh chervil or parsley
225g/8oz/1 cup butter, softened
Salt and pepper

Cut the bacon in half lengthwise and again in half across. Peel the lemon grass and use only the core. Cut into small pieces. Place a piece of fish on each strip of bacon and top with a piece of lemon grass. Roll up. Thread the rolls of fish on skewers, alternating with peppers, mushrooms and bay leaves. Brush with oil and grill 15 minutes, turning and basting often. While the fish cooks, heat the white wine, vinegar and shallots in a small saucepan until boiling. Cook rapidly to reduce by half. Add the herbs and lower the heat. Beat in the softened butter a bit at a time until the sauce is the thickness of hollandaise sauce. Season with salt and pepper to taste and serve with the fish kebabs.

BARBECUED VEGETABLES

Grilled Fennel

PREPARATION TIME: 15 minutes

COOKING TIME: 20 minutes

SERVES: 4 people

4 small bulbs fennel
Juice and rind of 1 lemon
60ml/4 tbsps oil
1 shallot, finely chopped
Salt and pepper

Remove the fennel tops and reserve them. Cut the fennel bulbs in half and remove the cores. Parboil the fennel for 5 minutes. Combine the juice and rind of the lemon, salt, pepper, oil and shallot. Pour over the fennel and set aside for 15 minutes. Place the fennel bulbs on hot coals and cook 15 minutes, turning often and brushing with the lemon mixture. Chop the fennel tops finely and sprinkle over the grilled fennel. Pour over any remaining lemon juice mixture to serve.

Grilled Tomatoes

PREPARATION TIME: 15 minutes

COOKING TIME: 6 minutes

SERVES: 4 people

4 beefsteak tomatoes cut in half
15ml/1 tbsp oregano, fresh or dried
30ml/2 tbsps olive oil
15ml/1 tbsp lemon juice
Salt and pepper
120g/4oz feta cheese, crumbled

Mix the oil, lemon juice, salt, pepper and oregano together. Brush over the cut side of the tomatoes and grill that side first for 3 minutes over hot coals. Brush the skin side of the tomatoes and turn them over. Grill 3 minutes more on skin side and remove the tomatoes to a serving dish. Sprinkle over the crumbled feta cheese and pour over the remaining basting mixture to serve.

Grilled Corn-on-the-Cob

PREPARATION TIME: 20 minutes

COOKING TIME: 15 minutes

SERVES: 4 people

4 large ears of corn, husks and silk
  removed, parboiled 5 minutes
120g/4oz/½ cup butter, melted
Salt and pepper
Chili powder or paprika (optional)

Brush the drained corn liberally with melted butter. Sprinkle with salt and pepper. Chili powder or paprika can be substituted for the pepper, if desired. Grill over medium hot coals for 15 minutes, turning often and basting frequently with butter. To serve, pour over any remaining butter.

Grilled Aubergine/ Eggplant

PREPARATION TIME: 30 minutes

COOKING TIME: 20-24 minutes

SERVES: 4 people

2 aubergines/eggplants
180ml/6 fl oz/¾ cup olive oil
90ml/6 tbsps lemon juice
15ml/1 tbsp cumin seed
1 clove garlic, finely chopped
30ml/2 tbsps parsley, chopped
Salt and pepper

Cut the aubergine/eggplant into rounds about 2.5cm/1 inch thick. Score the surface of each round lightly with a sharp knife, sprinkle with salt and leave to stand for 30 minutes. Heat oil for 1 minute and add the cumin seed and cook for the 30 seconds. Add the garlic and cook for a further 30 seconds. Add the lemon juice. Rinse the salt from the aubergine/eggplant slices and pat dry. Brush one side of the slices with the basting mixture. Grill on a lightly oiled rack or place in a hinged wire rack. Cook for 10-12 minutes per side until soft, basting frequently. Place the slices in a serving dish and pour over the remaining basting mixture. Sprinkle with parsley just before serving.

Grilled Mushrooms

PREPARATION TIME: 10 minutes

COOKING TIME: 15-20 minutes

SERVES: 4 people

450g/1lb large mushrooms, cleaned

MARINADE
15ml/1 tbsp chopped tarragon, fresh or
  dried
Grated rind and juice of 1 orange
15ml/1 tbsp tarragon vinegar
30ml/2 tbsps oil
Salt and pepper

**Facing page: Grilled Tomatoes
(top), and Grilled Fennel (bottom).**

Mix together the marinade ingredients. Cut the stalks from the mushrooms and place the mushroom caps in a shallow dish. Pour over the marinade and leave the mushrooms for 15-20 minutes. Place the mushrooms in a wire rack and cook 15-20 minutes over hot coals. Brush the mushrooms frequently with the marinade and turn them once or twice. Remove to a serving dish and pour over the remaining marinade to serve.

Courgette/Zucchini, Pepper and Onion Kebabs

| **PREPARATION TIME:** 20 minutes |
| **COOKING TIME:** 10-12 minutes |
| **SERVES:** 4 people |

4-6 courgettes/zucchini, ends trimmed
1 large onion
1 large green pepper
1 large red pepper
Oil
60ml/4 tbsps dry white wine
5ml/1 tsp thyme
10ml/2 tsps chopped parsley
5ml/1 tsp chopped chives
120g/4oz/½ cup melted butter

Peel the courgettes/zucchini with swivel peeler for a striped effect. Parboil 4 minutes. Refresh under cold water. Cut in 5cm/2 inch pieces. Quarter the onion and cut in large pieces, separating the layers. Cut the peppers in half and remove the core and seeds. Cut into pieces the same size as the onion. Thread the vegetables onto skewers. Melt the butter and add the wine and cook 1 minute. Add the herbs, salt and pepper. Brush the kebabs lightly with oil and grill 5-6 minutes per side. Brush frequently with the butter mixture. When the courgettes/zucchini are tender, remove to a serving dish. Pour over the remaining butter.

Barbecued Baked Potatoes

| **PREPARATION TIME:** 15 minutes |
| **COOKING TIME:** 25 minutes |
| **SERVES:** 4-6 people |

4 large potatoes, scrubbed but not peeled
Salt and pepper
Paprika
120g/4oz/½ cup melted butter

SAUCE
280ml/½ pint/1 cup sour cream
10ml/2 tsps red wine vinegar

This page: Courgette/Zucchini, Pepper and Onion Kebabs. Facing page: Grilled Aubergine/Eggplant and Grilled Mushrooms.

5ml/1 tsp sugar
5ml/1 tsp mustard powder
5ml/1 tsp celery salt
5ml/1 tsp chopped fresh herbs

Parboil the potatoes for 10 minutes in their skins. Cut the potatoes in quarters lengthwise. Brush the potatoes with a mixture of butter, paprika, salt and pepper on all surfaces. Grill the potatoes for 15 minutes, basting frequently with the remaining butter. Meanwhile, combine all the sauce ingredients and set aside in the refrigerator until ready to serve with the potatoes.

This page: Grilled Corn-on-the-Cob (top), and Barbecued Baked Potatoes (bottom). Facing page: Hungarian Sausage Salad.

MAIN COURSE SALADS

Hungarian Sausage Salad

PREPARATION TIME: 25 minutes

COOKING TIME: 20-25 minutes

SERVES: 4-6 people

4 small potatoes
140ml/¼ pint/½ cup oil
45ml/3 tbsps wine vinegar
5ml/1 tsp Dijon mustard
5ml/1 tsp dill seeds, slightly crushed
15ml/1 tbsp chopped parsley
5ml/1 tsp chopped dill
Pinch hot paprika
Salt
450g/1lb sausage such as kielbasa,
  smoked pork sausage, knockwurst or
  bratwurst
1 large red onion, thinly sliced
2 green peppers, cored and sliced
4 tomatoes, quartered

Scrub and peel potatoes and cook in salted water in a covered saucepan for 20 minutes or until soft. Mix all the dressing ingredients together in a medium-sized bowl. Dice the potatoes while still warm and coat with the dressing. Leave the potatoes to cool in the dressing. If using knockwurst boil for 5 minutes. Grill/broil the bratwurst until evenly browned on all sides. Slice the sausage in 2.5cm/½ inch slices and combine with the onion, pepper and tomatoes. Carefully combine with the potatoes in the dressing, taking care not to over mix and break up the potatoes. Pile into a large serving dish and allow to stand for 1 hour before serving.

Salade Niçoise

PREPARATION TIME: 20 minutes

COOKING TIME: 15-20 minutes

SERVES: 4 people

2 large potatoes, or 6 small new potatoes
180g/6oz French/green beans
4 hard-boiled eggs
1 can tuna
120g/4oz prawns/shrimp
1 can anchovies
4 ripe tomatoes
90g/3oz/¾ cup black olives, stoned
1 small cucumber, diced

DRESSING
90ml/6 tbsps olive oil
30ml/2 tbsps white wine vinegar

45ml/3 tbsps chopped mixed fresh herbs
10ml/2 tsps French mustard
Salt and pepper

Peel and cook the potatoes (skins may be left on new potatoes if desired) until tender. If using old potatoes, cut into 1.25cm/½ inch dice (new potatoes may be sliced into 6mm/¼ inch rounds). Trim the ends of the beans, put into boiling salted water for about 3-4 minutes or until just barely cooked. Drain and rinse under cold water, then leave to drain dry. Quarter the tomatoes, or if large cut into eighths. Quarter the hard-boiled eggs. Cut the anchovies into short strips. Mix the dressing ingredients together and blend well. Drain oil from the tuna and mix the tuna and all the salad ingredients together. Pour over the dressing and toss carefully, so that the potatoes do not break up. Serve the salad on top of lettuce leaves if desired.

Salade Bresse

PREPARATION TIME: 20 minutes

SERVES: 4-6 people

1 bunch lamb's lettuce or watercress, washed
1 head radicchio, leaves separated and washed
1 head cos/romaine lettuce, washed
4 chicken breasts, cooked, skinned and thinly sliced
120g/4oz Bresse Bleu or other blue cheese, cut in small pieces
16 cornichons (small pickled gherkins) thinly sliced
120g/4oz cherry tomatoes, halved and cored
60g/2oz/½ cup walnut halves

DRESSING

30ml/2 tbsps vegetable and walnut oil mixed
10ml/2 tsps white wine vinegar
180ml/6 fl oz/¾ cup crème fraîche
10ml/2 tsps chopped fresh tarragon
Salt and pepper

Tear the radicchio and cos/romaine lettuce into bite-size pieces. Leave the lamb's lettuce in whole leaves. If using watercress, remove the thick stems and yellow leaves. Toss the lettuces together and pile onto a salad plate. Place the chicken, cheese, cornichons, tomatoes and walnuts on top of the lettuce. Mix the oils and vinegar together and whisk well to emulsify. Fold in the crème fraîche and add the tarragon, salt and pepper. Drizzle some of the dressing over the salad to serve and hand the rest of the dressing separately.

Pasta and Vegetables in Parmesan Dressing

PREPARATION TIME: 25 minutes

COOKING TIME: 13-15 minutes

SERVES: 6 people

450g/1lb pasta spirals or other shapes
225g/8oz assorted vegetables such as:
Courgettes/zucchini, cut in rounds or matchsticks
Broccoli, trimmed into very small flowerets

This page: Salade Niçoise (top), and Salade Bresse (bottom). Facing page: Pasta and Vegetables in Parmesan Dressing.

Mangetout/pea pods, ends trimmed
Carrots, cut in rounds or matchsticks
Celery, cut in matchsticks
Cucumber, cut in matchsticks
Spring/green onions, thinly shredded or
  sliced
Asparagus tips
French/green beans, sliced
Red or yellow peppers, thinly sliced

DRESSING
140ml/¼ pint/½ cup olive oil
45ml/3 tbsps lemon juice
15ml/1 tbsp sherry pepper sauce
15ml/1 tbsp chopped parsley
15ml/1 tbsp chopped basil
60g/2oz/¼ cup freshly grated Parmesan
  cheese
30ml/2 tbsps mild mustard
Salt and pepper
Pinch sugar

Cook pasta in a large saucepan of boiling salted water with 15ml/1 tbsp oil for 10-12 minutes or until just tender. Rinse under hot water to remove starch. Leave in cold water. Place all the vegetables except the cucumber into boiling salted water for 3 minutes until just tender. Rinse in cold water and leave to drain. Mix the dressing ingredients together very well. Drain the pasta thoroughly and toss with the dressing. Add the vegetables and toss to coat. Refrigerate for up to 1 hour before serving.

Cob Salad

PREPARATION TIME: 25 minutes

SERVES: 4-6 people

1 large head cos/romaine lettuce, washed
2 avocados, peeled and chopped
3 tomatoes, cut in small dice
1 cucumber, cut in small dice
120g/4 oz/1 cup blue cheese, crumbled
4 spring/green onions, chopped or 1 small
  red onion, chopped
120g/4 oz cooked chicken breasts, cut in
  small pieces
2 hard-boiled eggs, chopped

GREEN GODDESS DRESSING
½ can anchovies
60ml/4 tbsps chopped parsley
30ml/2 tbsps chopped basil or tarragon

30ml/2 tbsps chopped chives
Small bunch watercress, leaves only
430ml/¾ pint/1½ cups mayonnaise
15ml/1 tbsp white wine vinegar

Dry the lettuce and cut it into strips. Tear the strips into small pieces and put into a salad bowl. Arrange all the ingredients on top. To prepare the dressing, combine all the ingredients in the blender or food processor and purée until smooth and very green. Serve the dressing separately with the salad.

Crab Louis

PREPARATION TIME: 20 minutes

SERVES: 4 people

DRESSING
280ml/½ pint/1 cup mayonnaise
120ml/4 fl oz/½ cup yogurt
60ml/4 tbsps tomato chutney/chili sauce
2 spring/green onions, finely chopped
½ green pepper, finely diced
5ml/1 tsp lemon juice
Salt and pepper

450g/1lb crabmeat, flaked
1 head Buttercrunch or ½ head Iceberg
  lettuce
4 hard-boiled eggs, quartered
120g/4oz/1 cup black olives, stoned

Combine all the dressing ingredients and mix half with the flaked crabmeat. Arrange a bed of lettuce on a serving dish and mound on the crabmeat. Coat the crabmeat with the remaining dressing. Arrange the quartered egg and black olives around the salad.

Julienne Salad

PREPARATION TIME: 25 minutes

SERVES: 4-6 people

1 small head Iceberg lettuce
1 small Buttercrunch lettuce
4 tomatoes, quartered
1 small red onion, chopped
½ cucumber, sliced
6 radishes, sliced
60g/2oz cooked ham
60g/2oz cooked tongue

120g/4oz cooked chicken
60g/2oz Gruyère or Swiss cheese
60g/2oz Red Leicester/Colby cheese

CREAMY HERB DRESSING
280ml/½ pint/1 cup natural yogurt
120ml/4 fl oz/½ cup double/heavy
  cream
45ml/3 tbsps fresh mixed herbs, chopped
  (use chervil, tarragon, basil, dill or
  parsley)
30ml/2 tbsps prepared mayonnaise
Salt and pepper

Tear the lettuce into bite-sized pieces and mix with the remaining vegetables. Divide into four salad bowls. Slice the meats and the cheeses into thin strips. Arrange on top of the salad ingredients. Mix the dressing thoroughly and serve separately.

Lobster and Cauliflower Salad

PREPARATION TIME: 30 minutes

SERVES: 4-6 people

1 large cauliflower, washed
140ml/¼ pint/½ cup vegetable oil
45ml/3 tbsps lemon juice
5ml/1 tsp dry mustard
Salt and pepper
1 large cooked lobster
280ml/½ pint/1 cup prepared
  mayonnaise
10ml/2 tsps Dijon mustard
4 hard-boiled eggs
16 black olives, halved and stoned
2 bunches watercress, washed
Red caviar

Break the cauliflower into small flowerets and mix with the vegetable oil, lemon juice, mustard and salt and pepper. Leave for at least 2 hours in a cool place. Crack the lobster and remove all the meat from the shell and set aside in a small bowl. Mix the mayonnaise and Dijon mustard. Thin if necessary with a spoonful of hot water. Add half the dressing to the

**Facing page: Julienne Salad (top),
and Cob Salad (bottom).**

lobster and mix carefully. Combine the cauliflower with the eggs and olives. Stir to coat the eggs with dressing but do not over-mix or break up the eggs. Remove the thick stems from the watercress and any yellow leaves. Arrange beds of watercress on four small plates. Spoon in equal portions of the cauliflower salad onto the watercress and top with an equal portion of the

lobster. Coat the lobster salads with the remaining mustard mayonnaise and spoon some red caviar over the dressing.

Tuna and Pasta with Red Kidney Beans

PREPARATION TIME: 20 minutes

This page: Tuna and Pasta with Red Kidney Beans. Facing page: Crab Louis (top), and Lobster and Cauliflower Salad (bottom).

COOKING TIME: 10 minutes

SERVES: 4-6 people

225g/8oz/1½ cups small pasta shells
1 225g/8oz can red kidney beans,
  drained and rinsed

120g/4oz small mushrooms, quartered
1 can tuna, drained and flaked
4 spring/green onions, sliced
30ml/2 tbsps chopped mixed herbs

DRESSING
140ml/¼ pint/½ cup olive oil
45ml/3 tbsps white wine vinegar
Squeeze lemon juice
15ml/1 tbsp Dijon mustard
Salt and pepper

Cook the pasta shells in boiling salted water with 15ml/1 tbsp oil for 10 minutes or until just tender. Rinse under hot water and then place in cold water until ready to use. Mix the dressing ingredients together thoroughly and drain the pasta shells. Mix the pasta with the beans, mushrooms, tuna, spring/green onions and chopped mixed herbs. Pour over the dressing and toss to coat. Chill up to 1 hour in the refrigerator before serving.

Mariner's Salad

PREPARATION TIME: 25 minutes
COOKING TIME: 15 minutes
SERVES: 6 people

450g/1lb pasta shells, plain and spinach
4 large scallops, cleaned
280ml/½ pint/1 cup frozen mussels, defrosted
140ml/¼ pint/½ cup lemon juice and water mixed
120g/4oz shelled and de-veined prawns/ shrimp
140ml/¼ pint/½ cup cockles or small clams, cooked
4 crab sticks, cut in small pieces
4 spring/green onions, chopped
15ml/1 tbsp chopped parsley

DRESSING
Grated rind and juice of ½ lemon
280ml/½ pint/1 cup mayonnaise
10ml/2 tsps paprika
90ml/3 fl oz/⅓ cup sour cream or natural yogurt
Salt and pepper

Cook the pasta for 10 minutes in a large pan of boiling salted water with 15ml/1 tbsp oil. Drain and rinse under hot water. Leave in cold water

until ready to use. Cook the scallops and mussels in the lemon juice and water mixture for about 5 minutes or until fairly firm. Cut the scallops into 2 or 3 pieces, depending upon size. Mix the dressing and drain the pasta thoroughly. Mix all ingredients together to coat completely with dressing. Stir carefully so that the shellfish do not break-up. Chill for up to 1 hour before serving.

Italian Pasta Salad

PREPARATION TIME: 25 minutes
COOKING TIME: 10 minutes
SERVES: 4-6 people

450g/1lb pasta shapes
225g/8oz assorted Italian meats, cut in strips: salami, mortadella, prosciutto, coppa, bresaola
120g/4oz provolone or fontina cheese, cut in strips
15 black olives, halved and stoned
60g/4 tbsp small capers
120g/4oz peas
1 small red onion or 2 shallots, chopped
160g/6oz oyster mushrooms, stems trimmed and sliced

DRESSING
45ml/3 tbsps white wine vinegar
140ml/¼ pint/½ cup olive oil
½ clove garlic, minced
5ml/1 tsp fennel seed, crushed
15ml/1 tbsp chopped parsley
15ml/1 tbsp chopped basil
15ml/1 tbsp mustard
Salt and pepper

Cook the pasta in a large saucepan of boiling water with a pinch of salt and 15ml/1 tbsp oil. Cook for about 10 minutes or until just tender. Add the frozen peas during the last 3 minutes of cooking time. Drain the pasta and peas and rinse under hot water. Leave in cold water until ready to use. Mix the dressing ingredients together well and drain the pasta and peas thoroughly. Mix the pasta and peas with the Italian meats and cheeses, olives, capers, chopped onion or shallot and sliced mushrooms. Pour the dressing over the salad and toss all the ingredients together to coat. Do not over-mix.

Leave the salad to chill for up to 1 hour before serving.

Shrimp and Cashews in Pineapples with Tarragon Dressing

PREPARATION TIME: 30 minutes
COOKING TIME: 10 minutes
SERVES: 4 people

2 small fresh pineapples
225g/8oz small cooked shrimp
120g/4oz/1 cup roasted unsalted cashew nuts
2 sticks celery, thinly sliced
60ml/4 tbsps lemon juice

DRESSING
1 egg
30ml/2 tbsps sugar
15ml/1 tbsp tarragon vinegar
120ml/4 fl oz/¼ pint whipping cream
10ml/2 tsps chopped fresh tarragon or 5ml/1 tsp dried tarragon, crumbled

Cut the pineapples carefully in half lengthwise, leaving the green tops attached. Carefully cut out the flesh and remove the cores. Cut the flesh into bite-size pieces. Combine the shrimp, cashews and celery and toss with the lemon juice. Spoon the mixture into the pineapple shells and refrigerate to chill. To prepare the dressing, beat the egg and sugar together until light in a heat-proof bowl. Add the vinegar and tarragon, place the bowl over hot water. Whip with a wire whisk until thick. Take off the heat and allow to cool, whisking occasionally. When cold, lightly whip the cream and fold into the dressing. Spoon over the salad and serve in the pineapple shells.

Facing page: Italian Pasta Salad (top), and Mariner's Salad (bottom).

Oriental Salad

PREPARATION TIME: 25 minutes

COOKING TIME: 2 minutes

SERVES: 4-6 people

1 cake tofu, cut in small cubes
140ml/¼ pint/½ cup vegetable oil
120g/4oz mangetout/pea pods, ends
*   trimmed*
60g/2oz mushrooms, sliced
60g/2oz broccoli flowerets
2 carrots, peeled and thinly sliced
4 spring/green onions thinly sliced
2 sticks celery, thinly sliced
60g/2oz/½ cup unsalted roasted peanuts

120g/4oz bean sprouts
½ head Chinese leaves/cabbage, shredded

DRESSING
45ml/3 tbsps lemon juice
10ml/2 tsps honey
5ml/1 tsp grated ginger
45ml/3 tbsps soy sauce
Dash sesame oil

Drain tofu well and press gently to remove excess moisture. Cut into 1.25cm/½ inch cubes. Heat 30ml/ 2 tbsps from the 140ml/¼ pint/ ½ cup oil in the wok or frying pan. Save the remaining oil for the dressing. Cook the mangetout/pea

This page: Oriental Salad. Facing page: Shrimps and Cashews in Pineapple with Tarragon Dressing.

pods, mushrooms, broccoli, carrots and celery for 2 minutes. Remove the vegetables and set them aside to cool. When cool mix them together with the onions, peanuts and bean sprouts. Mix the dressing and pour over the vegetables. Add the tofu and toss carefully. Arrange a bed of Chinese leaves/cabbage on a serving dish and pile the salad ingredients on top to serve.

SALADS WITH FRUIT

Waldorf Salad

PREPARATION TIME: 20 minutes

SERVES: 6 people

4 sticks celery, diced
4 apples, mixture of red-skinned and
  green-skinned, diced
180g/6oz grapes, black and white, halved
  and seeded
120g/4oz/1 cup walnuts or pecans,
  roughly chopped
280ml/½ pint/1 cup prepared
  mayonnaise
60ml/4 tbsps heavy cream
Juice of half a lemon

Mix the celery, apples, grapes and
nuts together and toss with the
lemon juice. Lightly whip the cream,
fold into the mayonnaise. Fold the
dressing into the salad and serve
chilled. If desired, substitute raisins
for the grapes and garnish with
30ml/2 tbsps chopped parsley.

Fruit Salad with Coconut Cream Dressing

PREPARATION TIME: 30 minutes

SERVES: 6-8 people

900g/2lb fresh assorted fruit, such as:
Pineapple, peeled, cored and cut in
  wedges
Melon, skinned and sliced
Bananas, peeled, cut in thick rounds and
  sprinkled with lemon juice
Apricots, halved and stoned and sprinkled
  with lemon juice
Peaches, peeled and sliced and sprinkled
  with lemon juice
Strawberries, hulled and washed
Raspberries or blackberries washed

Papaya, peeled and sliced
Currants, stems removed
Blueberries/bilberries, washed
Kiwi, peeled and sliced
Kumquats, thinly sliced, seeds removed
Fresh figs, quartered
Pears, peeled, cored and sliced

DRESSING
280ml/½ pint/1 cup natural yogurt
140ml/¼ pint/½ cup coconut cream
30-45ml/2-3 tbsps lime juice
Seeds of 1 fresh pomegranate

Arrange assortment of fruit on
plates. Mix together the ingredients
for the dressing and drizzle over the
fruit. Sprinkle on the pomegranate
seeds.

Green and Gold Sunflower Salad

PREPARATION TIME: 15 minutes

SERVES: 4 people

2 large ripe avocados
8 ripe apricots

DRESSING
45ml/3 tbsps sunflower oil
15ml/1 tbsp lemon juice
Salt and pepper

YOGURT DRESSING
140ml/¼ pint/½ cup natural yogurt
10ml/2 tsps honey
Grated rind of 1 lemon
10ml/2 tsps chopped parsley
60g/4 tbsps toasted sunflower seeds
1 small Buttercrunch lettuce, washed and
  separated into leaves

Prepare the oil and lemon juice
dressing. Cut avocados in half and
remove the stones. Peel and cut into
slices. Cut apricots in half and

remove the stones. If the apricots are
large cut in half again. Add the
apricots to the avocados, spooning
over the dressing. Mix all the
ingredients for the yogurt dressing
together except the sunflower seeds.
Place the lettuce leaves on salad
plates and arrange the avocado and
apricots on top. Spoon over some of
the yogurt dressing and sprinkle the
sunflower seeds onto the dressing.
Serve immediately and hand extra
dressing separately.

Watercress and Orange Salad

PREPARATION TIME: 20 minutes

SERVES: 4-6 people

3 large bunches watercress, well washed
  and thick stalks removed
4 oranges, peeled and segmented

DRESSING
90ml/6 tbsps vegetable oil
Juice and rind of 1 orange
Pinch sugar
Squeeze lemon juice
Salt and pepper

Break watercress into small sprigs
and discard any yellow leaves.
Arrange the watercress with the
orange segments on plates or toss in
one large salad bowl. Mix the
dressing ingredients together very
well and pour over the salad just
before serving.

**Facing page: Watercress and
Orange Salad (top), and Waldorf
Salad (bottom).**

Fennel, Orange and Tomato Salad

PREPARATION TIME: 25 minutes

COOKING TIME: 3-4 minutes

SERVES: 4 people

2 bulbs fennel, green top trimmed and
*   reserved*
2 large, ripe tomatoes
2 oranges

DRESSING
30ml/2 tbsps orange juice
25ml/1½ tbsps lemon juice
Zest of 1 orange
90ml/3 fl oz/⅓ cup olive oil and
*   vegetable oil mixed half and half*
5ml/1 tsp chopped fresh oregano or basil

Pinch sugar
Salt and pepper

Choose fennel with a lot of feathery green top. Reserve the tops. Cut the cores out of the bottom of the fennel bulbs and discard. Bring water to the boil in a large saucepan. Slice the fennel thinly, lengthwise, and place the slices in the boiling water. Cook until becoming translucent and slightly softened, about 3-4 minutes. Carefully remove the slices to a colander and rinse under cold water. Leave to drain. Place the tomatoes into the boiling water for 5-10 seconds. Put immediately into cold water. Peel and slice into 6mm/ ¼ inch rounds. Grate or use a zester to remove the peel from 1 orange.

This page: Fruit Salad with Coconut Cream Dressing. Facing page: Green and Gold Sunflower Salad (top), and Fennel, Orange and Tomato Salad (bottom).

Peel off the pith with knife and peel the remaining orange. Slice both oranges into 6mm/¼ inch rounds. Prepare the dressing by whisking all the ingredients very well and reserving the orange zest. Arrange the fennel, tomato and orange slices in circles on a round serving dish. Pour over the dressing and sprinkle on the orange zest. Chop the fennel tops and sprinkle over or use whole to garnish the salad.

SUMMER DESSERTS

Gooseberry Pie

PREPARATION TIME: 20 minutes

COOKING TIME: 1 hour

OVEN: 220°C (425°F) Gas Mark 7 for 30 minutes, then 180°C (350°F) Gas Mark 4 for 30 minutes

Pastry
275g (10oz) plain flour
Pinch of salt
65g (2½oz) butter (cut into small pieces)
65g (2½oz) lard (cut into small pieces)
2½ tablespoons cold water

Filling
900g (2lb) gooseberries, topped and tailed
225g (8oz) granulated sugar
Milk to glaze or beaten egg
Single cream or custard

Pastry
Sift the flour with the salt. Add the fat and mix until it resembles breadcrumbs. Stir in the water and form into a firm dough. Roll out half the pastry on a lightly floured surface and use it to line a 20cm (8 inch) flan dish or pie dish.

Filling
Mix the gooseberries with the sugar and fill the lined pastry dish. Roll out the remaining pastry and cover the pie. Dampen the edges and seal together. Any excess pastry can be used to make leaves to decorate. Make a small hole in the centre of the pie and brush the pastry with milk or beaten egg. Place on baking tray and cook in a hot oven. Serve with single cream or custard.

Melons and Mangoes on Ice

PREPARATION TIME: 1¼ hours

1 medium size Ogen melon
2 large mangoes

Slice melon in half and scoop out flesh in balls. Peel mangoes and slice. Mix mango slices and melon balls together and arrange in a glass bowl. Chill for 1 hour.

Frozen Gooseberry Fool

PREPARATION TIME: 20 minutes
plus freezing

COOKING TIME: 15 minutes

650g (1½lb) gooseberries
450ml (¾ pint) water
Sprig of mint
150g (6 oz) caster sugar
A little green food colouring
450ml (¾ pint) double cream, lightly whipped

Top and tail gooseberries. Place in a pan with the water and mint. Cover and simmer for approximately 15 minutes or until soft. Take off the heat and stir in the sugar until dissolved, then add food colouring. Take out the sprig of mint. Sieve and ensure all pips are removed. Cool and blend with the cream. Place in container and freeze.

Brown Bread Ice Cream

PREPARATION TIME: 20 minutes
plus freezing

475ml (17 fl oz) vanilla ice cream
4 small slices brown bread
1 teaspoon ground cinnamon
125ml (4 fl oz) water
75g (3oz) sugar

Put the ice cream into a large mixing bowl and break it up, allowing it to soften. Cut the crusts from the bread and discard. Crumble the slices into a bowl, adding the ground cinnamon, reserve. Put the water and sugar into a small saucepan and stir until the sugar has dissolved. Boil until the mixture caramelises and turns brown. Remove from the heat and stir in the breadcrumbs and cinnamon mixture. Blend the mixture into the ice cream, making sure the breadcrumbs do not form large lumps. Turn the mixture into a rigid container for freezing, (leave 10mm (½ inch) space at the top of the container). Freeze the mixture and serve.

Brown Bread Ice-Cream (top left), Melons and Mangoes on Ice (top right), Frozen Gooseberry Fool (bottom left) and Gooseberry Pie (bottom right).

Cherry 'Spoom'

PREPARATION TIME: 20 minutes
plus freezin

250g (9oz) sugar
300ml (½ pint) water
Juice of 2 limes
2 fresh peppermint leaves
600ml (1 pint) Sauternes
3 egg whites
Cherry brandy

Boil 100g (4oz) of the sugar with
the water, lime juice and
peppermint leaves. Leave to cool
and strain into the Sauternes.
Freeze the sorbet. Whisk the egg
whites and add the remaining suga
until it peaks. Remove the sorbet
from the freezer and whisk in the
meringue mixture. Serve in glasses
and pour over the cherry brandy.

Apple and Sultana and Brandy Ice

PREPARATION TIME: 10 minutes
plus soaking and freezing time

600ml (1 pint) apple juice
50g (2oz) caster sugar
42g (1½oz) packet dried apple flakes
100g (4oz) sultanas
A few drops green food colour
1 egg white, stiffly whisked

Put the apple juice in a pan with
sugar. Heat gently until the sugar
has dissolved. Boil quickly for 5
minutes and remove from heat.
Cool. Soak apple flakes and
sultanas in brandy and add enough
apple syrup to cover mixture. Soak
for 4 hours. Then mix apple,
sultanas and brandy adding a few
drops of food colour mixture with
the remaining apple syrup in a
shallow container and freeze. Mask
with a fork and fold in egg whites.
Return to the freezer. Serve frozen
in glasses.

This page: **Burgundy Granita**
(top), Apple and Sultana and
Brandy Ice (centre) and
Champagne Granita
(bottom).

Facing page: **Cherry 'Spoom'**
(top), Raspberry Malakoff
(centre) and Cherry
Cinnamon Sorbet (bottom).

Burgundy Granita

PREPARATION TIME: 15 minutes
plus freezing

75g (3oz) sugar, plus 2 tablespoons
Juice of ½ lime and ½ orange
1 tablespoon water
Small bunch lemon balm leaves
½ bottle good Burgundy
125ml (4 fl oz) double or whipping
   cream
Blackberries to decorate

Boil half the sugar with the lime and orange juice and water, and the balm leaves. Cool, strain and add to Burgundy. Freeze in a shallow container. To serve: whip the cream with the remaining sugar. Scrape the granita with a spoon to produce ice shavings and serve shavings into glasses, decorate with cream and blackberries.

Champagne Granita

PREPARATION TIME: 5 minutes
plus freezing time

⅔ bottle champagne
Fresh blackcurrants and raspberries
Caster sugar to dust

Freeze the champagne in a shallow container. When frozen, scrape off and serve into glasses. Decorate with blackcurrants and raspberries. Dust with caster sugar.

Raspberry Malakoff

PREPARATION TIME: 35 minutes
plus chilling

175g (6oz) caster sugar
175g (6oz) butter
300ml (½ pint) double cream
175g (6oz) ground almonds
3 tablespoons kirsch
225g (8oz) fresh raspberries
1 packet boudoir biscuits
Whipped cream

Beat the sugar and butter until fluffy. Whip the cream until it peaks and fold in the ground almonds. Add the kirsch and raspberries. Mix the sugar and butter with the cream fruit mixture. Line an 18cm (7 inch) cake tin with non-stick silicone paper. Stand the boudoir biscuits round the sides of the cake tin with the sugary side outermost. Spoon

the malakoff mixture into the middle and press it down. Make sure the top is smooth. Refrigerate until the malakoff feels firm. With a sharp knife, trim the biscuits to the same level as the malakoff mixture. Turn the malakoff out upside down. Decorate with whipped cream if desired. Serve chilled.

Cherry Cinnamon Sorbet

PREPARATION TIME: 25 minutes
plus freezing

175g (10oz) sugar, plus 1 tablespoon
300ml (½ pint) water
1 piece cinnamon stick
500g (18oz) fresh sour cherries
Juice of ½ lemon
200ml (7 fl oz) whipping cream
Seeds of ¼ vanilla pod
Fresh cherries

Boil 175g (10oz) of the sugar for 3 minutes in water and cinnamon and leave to cool. Remove the cinnamon sticks and stone the cherries. Purée the cherries and stir in the lemon juice. Mix with the sugar syrup and freeze. Flavour the cream with the tablespoon of sugar and vanilla. Whip until thick. Put the sorbet into individual glasses and decorate with cream and cherries.

Strawberry Alaska

PREPARATION TIME: 10 minutes
COOKING TIME: 2-3 minutes
OVEN: 140°C (275°F) Gas Mark 1

1 shop-bought strawberry jam swiss
   roll
Soft-scoop strawberry ice cream to
   cover

Meringue
2 egg whites
100g (4oz) caster sugar

Cover swiss roll with ice cream. Return to freezer. Whisk egg whites until they form stiff peaks. Whisk in half the sugar. Then fold in the rest. Remove ice cream covered swiss roll from freezer and cover with meringue mixture. Place in oven and cook meringue until just turning golden. (Approximately 2-3 minutes.) Serve immediately.

Strawberry Yogurt Ice

PREPARATION TIME: 20 minutes
plus freezing

225g (8oz) fresh or thawed, frozen
   strawberries
300ml (½ pint) plain low fat yogurt
2 teaspoons gelatine
2 tablespoons water
1 egg white
65g (2½oz) caster sugar
A few strawberries

Blend strawberries and yogurt until smooth. Sprinkle gelatine over the water in a small bowl. Place bowl in a pan of hot water until the gelatine is dissolved. Cool slightly and add to the strawberry mixture. Pour into the container and freeze until icy round the edges. Put mixture into bowl and beat until smooth. In another bowl whisk the egg white stiffly, carefully adding the sugar and fold into strawberry mixture. Pour back into container and freeze. To serve – scoop into glasses and decorate with strawberries.

Peach Melba

PREPARATION TIME: 10 minutes

1 large can peaches (2 halves per
   person)
2 scoops ice cream per person
Chocolate sauce or raspberry purée
Flaked almonds

Place 2 scoops of ice cream per serving in individual bowls. Place 2 peach halves on top. Serve with chocolate sauce or raspberry purée. Decorate with flaked almonds.

Lemon Sorbet

PREPARATION TIME: 15 minutes
plus freezing

Grated rinds and juice of 2 lemons
Cold water
75g (3oz) caster sugar
1 teaspoon gelatine
2 egg whites

Mix the lemon juice and rind with cold water to make 1 litre (1¾ pints) of fluid. Put the liquid in a saucepan with the sugar and boil. Remove from the heat and whisk in the gelatine. Pour into a mixing

bowl and place in the freezer until it begins to harden. Whisk the egg whites until stiff and beat them into the lemon mixture. Return to the freezer, leaving a 10mm (½ inch) head space in the container.

Pastel Coupé

PREPARATION TIME: 35 minutes
plus freezing

Yellow
600ml (1 pint) water
2 level teaspoons gelatine
250g (10oz) caster sugar
3 lemons
2 egg whites

Green
600ml (1 pint) water
2 level teaspoons gelatine
200g (8oz) caster sugar
2 lemons
2 egg whites
2 tablespoons crème de menthe

Yellow
Measure out two tablespoons of water and sprinkle with gelatine. Place the remaining water and sugar in a saucepan. Add pared lemon rinds and stir over the heat until the sugar has dissolved. Bring to the boil and simmer for 5 minutes. Remove from heat and add gelatine mixture. Dissolve completely and stir in the lemon juice. Leave to cool. Strain the mixture into a container and freeze until partially frozen. Place in chilled mixing bowl and whisk with beaten egg whites until thick and snowy. Return to container and freeze.

Green
For the green pastel coupé use basic method and ingredients as listed. Add the crème de menthe with lemon juice. To serve: use an ice-cream scoop, take half the green and half the yellow into one scoop. Serve in meringue cases or glasses.

Facing page: Strawberry Yogurt Ice (top), Peach Melba (centre) and Strawberry Alaska (bottom).

Curaçao Granita with Champagne

PREPARATION TIME: 10 minutes
plus freezing

75g (3oz) sugar
150ml (¼ pint) water
Juice of 1 lime
Juice of 1 orange
3 tablespoons blue Curaçao
⅔ bottle champagne

Boil half the sugar with the water, lime and orange juice for two to three minutes. Cool, strain, add to the Curaçao and the champagne. Pour into a flat freezer-proof container and freeze. To serve: scrape with a spoon and serve in glasses.

Blackcurrant Sorbet

PREPARATION TIME: 20 minutes
plus freezing

1kg (2lb) fresh or thawed, frozen
   blackcurrants
225g (9oz) sugar
300ml (½ pint) water
2 egg whites

Put all the ingredients except the egg whites into a saucepan. Heat slowly and cook for 15 minutes. Rub the fruit mixture through a sieve and pour into a freezer-proof container with a lid. Freeze until mushy. Whisk the egg whites until firm and fold into the mixture. Return to the freezer.

Inset illustration: (from top to bottom) Curaçao Granita with Champagne, Lemon Sorbet, Pastel Coupé and Blackcurrant Sorbet.

85

Ginger Syllabub

PREPARATION TIME: 15 minutes

1 100g (4oz) jar preserved ginger
600ml (1 pint) double cream, lightly
 whipped

Chop 2 pieces of the ginger and mix into the cream along with 2 tablespoons of the syrup. Serve in glasses or bowls and decorate with sliced ginger. Chill until ready to serve.

Apricot Ice Roll

PREPARATION TIME: 35 minutes
plus freezing

COOKING TIME: 12 minutes

OVEN: 220°C (425°F) Gas Mark 7

Sponge mixture
2 eggs
50g (2oz) caster sugar
50g (2oz) plain flour

Filling and decorating
4 tablespoons apricot jam
600ml (1 pint) soft-scoop ice cream
 (vanilla)
Cream to decorate
Dried apricots, thinly sliced

Whisk eggs and sugar until light and fluffy. Carefully fold in flour. Turn into a greased and floured swiss roll tin and bake. Turn out onto a tea towel and leave to cool. Spread sponge with apricot jam and softened ice cream. Roll up using tea towel. Place in freezer until ice cream is hardened. Decorate with cream and sliced apricots.

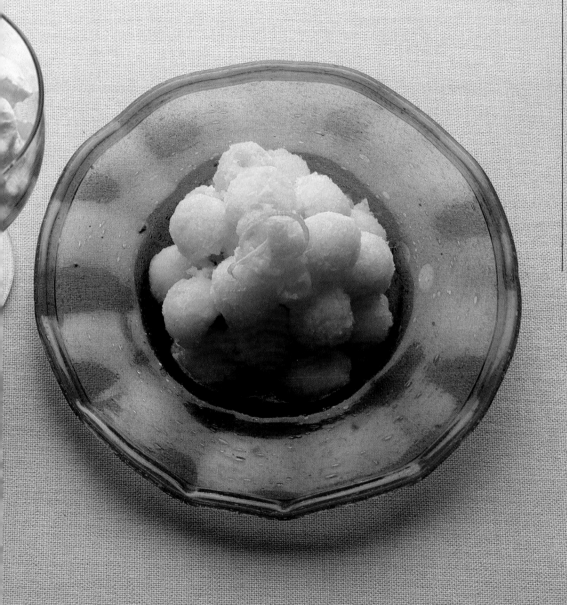

Mango Sorbet

PREPARATION TIME: 15 minutes
plus freezing

250ml (8 fl oz) mango purée
Juice of ½ lime
Scant 150ml (5 fl oz) dry white wine
Scant 150ml (5 fl oz) mineral water
1 egg white
50g (2oz) sugar

Mix the mango purée with the lime juice, white wine and mineral water. Whisk the egg white until it peaks and slowly add the sugar. Fold the egg white into the mango mixture and freeze.

Apricot Ice Roll (far left), Ginger Syllabub (centre) and Mango Sorbet (left).

Banana Ice Crêpes

PREPARATION TIME: 30 minutes

12 cooked crêpes
2 large bananas
12 scoops soft-scoop vanilla ice
 cream
Chocolate sauce

Mash one banana, and combine with ice cream. Fold the crêpes in half and place on individual plates. Fill crêpes with the mixture of banana and ice cream. Decorate with other sliced banana. Serve with chocolate sauce.

Mousse Glacée au Chocolat

PREPARATION TIME: 20 minutes
plus freezing

4 egg yolks
2 tablespoons caster sugar
2 teaspoons vanilla essence
300ml (½ pint) double cream
2 egg whites, stiffly whipped
Chocolate sauce

Whisk egg yolks and sugar until light and creamy. Add vanilla essence. Add the cream and egg whites. Freeze the mixture. Serve with chocolate sauce.

Chocolate Banana Ice

PREPARATION TIME: 35 minutes
plus freezing

150ml (¼ pint) milk
40g (1½oz) caster sugar
40g (1½oz) plain chocolate (broken
 into bits)
1 egg, beaten
½ teaspoon vanilla essence
150ml (¼ pint) double cream,
 whipped until soft peaking

Banana Cream
4 medium bananas
1 tablespoon lemon juice
25g (1oz) icing sugar, sieved
150ml (¼ pint) whipped double
 cream

Place the milk, sugar and chocolate in a saucepan and heat gently. Pour onto the beaten egg and stir constantly until mixed. Return the mixture to the saucepan and cook until the custard thickens. Strain the mixture, add the vanilla essence and allow to cool. Fold the cream into the custard mixture. Whisk rapidly and turn into a metal freezing container.

Banana Cream
Peel and chop the bananas and sprinkle with lemon juice. Dust the fruit with icing sugar and fold the whipped cream in with the bananas. Stir the chocolate mixture with banana cream and freeze. Remove from freezer to fridge 20 minutes before serving.

Refreshing Sorbet

PREPARATION TIME: 15 minutes
plus freezing

75g (3oz) caster sugar
425ml (¾ pint) water
3 ripe mangoes, peeled, stoned and
 mashed
Juice of 3 lemons
3 tablespoons white rum
3 egg whites, whisked

Over low heat, dissolve sugar in the water, boil for 10 minutes. Leave to cool. Blend mangoes with lemon juice and rum. Add the syrup. Pour into a container and freeze until just frozen. Turn into a bowl. Fold in the egg whites. Freeze.

Minted Lime Ice

PREPARATION TIME: 15 minutes
plus freezing

175g (6oz) caster sugar
375ml (12 fl oz) water
Grated rind and juice of 6 limes
4 tablespoons fresh mint, finely
 chopped
150ml (5 fl oz) double cream
3 tablespoons single cream

Place the sugar and water in a saucepan. Stir gently over a low heat. When the sugar has dissolved bring the mixture to the boil. Remove the pan from the heat. Stir in the grated rind of the limes. Add the juice and stir in the mint. Let the mixture cool and pour into ice trays. Freeze the mixture, covered with foil. When the mixture is frozen, crush it. Lightly whip the creams together. Stir the lime ice into the cream and re-freeze. Slightly thaw and spoon into small glasses to serve.

Lemon Ice Cream Sponge

PREPARATION TIME: 20 minutes
plus freezing

COOKING TIME: 15 minutes

OVEN: 220°C (425°F) Gas Mark 7

Sponge
3 large eggs
75g (3oz) caster sugar
75g (3oz) self raising flour, sieved

Filling
4 level teaspoons lemon curd
1 grated rind of lemon
6 scoops soft-scoop vanilla ice cream

To decorate
3 tablespoons double cream
Icing sugar
Sugared lemon slices

Sponge
Whisk eggs and sugar until light and fluffy. Sieve in flour and mix in carefully. Bake in a large 13cm (5 inch) baking tin. Turn out and cool.

Filling
Slice the cake into three horizontally. On bottom and middle slices spread lemon curd. Mix together the lemon rind and vanilla ice cream. Spread on top of the lemon curd. Sandwich together and freeze.

To decorate
Whip cream until stiff; place in piping bag with a star nozzle; pipe rosettes on top of the sponge. Dust with icing sugar and add lemon slices.

Custard Ice Cream

PREPARATION TIME: 20 minutes

5 egg yolks
150ml (¼ pint) single cream
150g (6oz) caster sugar
300ml (½ pint) double cream

Combine egg yolks, single cream and 100g (4oz) of the sugar in a basin. Place over a pan of simmering water and stir until mixture coats the back of a spoon. Strain mixture into a bowl and leave to cool. Whip double cream lightly. Mix with custard carefully. Fold in remaining 50g (2oz) of sugar. Pour into a freezer-proof container. Cover and freeze.

Coconut Sorbet

PREPARATION TIME: 20 minutes
plus freezin

250ml (8 fl oz) tinned coconut juice
Scant 150ml (5 fl oz) mineral water
2 tablespoons dark rum
2 egg whites
100g (4oz) sugar

To decorate
2 bananas, sliced
Chocolate sauce

Mix the coconut juice with the mineral water and rum. Whisk the egg whites until stiff, gradually adding the sugar. Stir the egg whites into the coconut mixture with a balloon whisk and freeze until creamy. Serve with banana slices and chocolate sauce.

Honey Ice Cream

PREPARATION TIME: 15 minutes
plus freezin

450g (1lb) raspberries
150ml (5 fl oz) clear honey
150ml (5 fl oz) double cream
2 tablespoons lemon juice
3 egg whites
120ml (4 fl oz) water
150ml (5 fl oz) single cream
4 x 15ml tablespoons granulated
 sugar

Cook the raspberries in a saucepa with the honey and water. Add th sugar and cook for 5 minutes unti dissolved. Leave to cool. Rub the mixture through a sieve and chill. Beat the double cream until thick and stir in the single cream. Fold the creams into the fruit mixture. Freeze until almost solid. Whisk and re-freeze.

Facing page: Mocha Soufflé (top), Chocolate Banana Ice (centre left), Banana Ice Crêpes (centre right) and Mousse Glacée au Chocolat (bottom).

Fancy Ice

PREPARATION TIME: 15 minutes

COOKING TIME: 10 minutes

OVEN: 220°C (425°F) Gas Mark 7

Sponge
2 eggs
50g (2oz) caster sugar
50g (2oz) flour

Topping
200g (8oz) fondant icing
1 tablespoon lemon juice
A few drops yellow food colour

Filling and decoration
Blackberry sorbet
Apricot purée
Blackberries

Sponge
Whisk eggs and caster sugar until light and fluffy. Sieve in the flour, fold gently into mixture. Lightly grease and flour a bun tin. Spoon into 12 portions and bake until golden brown. Turn out and cool on a wire rack.

Topping
Melt the fondant icing. Add the lemon juice and food colouring. Spoon over the cakes, leave to harden and set.

Filling and decoration
Fit a star nozzle on a piping bag and fill with blackberry sorbet. Cut the sponges in half and pipe onto top of base of cake; top with another. Serve with a spoonful of apricot purée on the side and decorate with blackberries.

Mocha Soufflé

PREPARATION TIME: 30 minutes
plus chilling

15g (½oz) gelatine
4 tablespoons warm water
25g (1oz) cocoa
1 teaspoon instant coffee
450ml (¾ pint) milk
4 eggs, separated
75g (3oz) caster sugar
2 tablespoons rum
150ml (5 fl oz) fresh double cream, whipped
Chocolate curls

Dissolve the gelatine in a small basin with the warm water. Mix the cocoa and coffee with the milk and bring to the boil in a saucepan. In a

mixing bowl beat the egg yolks and sugar together until pale and fluffy. Gradually beat in the milk mixture. Place the bowl over a saucepan of hot water for 15 minutes. Stir gently. Remove from heat and stir in the rum and dissolved gelatine. Allow to cool. Whisk the egg whites until they peak and fold into

the mixture. Mix in half of the double cream. Pour into a prepared ½ litre (1 pint) soufflé dish. Chill until set. Decorate with the remaining whipped cream and chocolate curls.

This page: Fancy Ice (top), Custard Ice Cream (centre) and Coconut Sorbet (bottom). Facing page: Refreshing Sorbet (top), Minted Lime Ice (centre left), Honey Ice Cream (centre right) and Lemon Ice Cream Sponge (bottom).

Avocado Cheese Balls (top), Celery Boats (above) and Prawn Stuffed Eggs (right).

PARTY SNACKS

Avocado Cheese Balls

PREPARATION TIME: 30 minutes + 30 minutes to refrigerate

MAKES: 25 party snacks

1 medium size, ripe avocado
15-30ml (1-2 tblsp) single cream or yoghurt
1 clove garlic, crushed (optional)
5ml (1 tsp) lemon juice
75g (3oz) finely grated low fat Cheddar cheese
5ml (1 tsp) made mustard
25g (1oz) fresh breadcrumbs
½ small onion, finely chopped
Freshly ground black pepper to taste
30ml (2 tblsp) freshly chopped parsley
50g (2oz) toasted almond nibs

Halve the avocado and twist apart. Remove stone. Peel each half. Mash the avocado flesh in a medium size mixing bowl. Add the cream or yoghurt, crushed garlic, lemon juice, grated cheese, mustard, breadcrumbs, onion and seasoning, mixing with a fork until a stiff paste results.
Using cold, damp hands, roll rounded teaspoons of the mixture into balls. Roll half in the finely chopped parsley to coat. Roll remaining balls in the cold, toasted nuts to coat.
Refrigerate for 30 minutes before serving.

Prawn Stuffed Eggs

PREPARATION TIME: 15 minutes

MAKES: 12 party snacks

6 eggs, size 4
50g (2oz) vegetable margarine or low fat spread
1 clove garlic, crushed
75g (3oz) cooked, peeled prawns, chopped
2.5ml (½ tsp) finely chopped basil
Freshley ground black pepper to taste
Low fat milk if necessary

Garnish:
Tiny pieces of red pepper
Bed of lettuce

Hard boil the eggs, stirring as they come to the boil. Drain and plunge immediately into cold water. Allow to cool completely. Shell and cut each egg in half

lengthwise. Remove yolks. Set aside.
Cream the margarine or low fat spread with the crushed clove of garlic. Beat in the egg yolks, prawns, basil and black pepper to taste. Add a little milk if necessary until a soft consistency results.
Fill the egg whites with the prepared mixtures. Serve garnished with a tiny piece of red pepper.
Note: This snack may be prepared in the morning provided it is kept airtight in the refrigerator until just before serving.

Celery Boats

PREPARATION TIME: 15-20 minutes

MAKES: 100 party snacks

2 heads celery, cleaned

For the Fish Paté:
2 medium size smoked mackerel fillets with peppercorns
100g (4oz) smoked salmon, chopped
Juice ½ lemon
100g (4oz) curd cheese
5ml (1 tsp) tomato purée
5ml (1 tsp) creamed horseradish
45ml (3 tblsp) thick-set natural yoghurt
1 tblsp fresh parsley sprigs

Garnish:
Sprigs of fresh mint
Lumpfish caviar

Make the paté. Skin the mackerel and flake the fish into the bowl of a food processor, using the metal blade, or into a liquidiser goblet. Process to chop finely — 5-7 seconds. Add the roughly chopped smoked salmon, the lemon juice, curd cheese, tomato purée, creamed horseradish, yoghurt, fresh parsley sprigs and seasoning. Process until smooth.
Cut the celery into boats and pipe or spread with the paté.
Garnish with the lumpfish caviar and sprigs of mint. Serve cold.
Note: This snack may be prepared in the morning provided it is kept airtight in the refrigerator until ready to serve.

Savoury Eclairs

PREPARATION TIME: 20-30 minutes

COOKING TIME: 20 minutes

MAKES: 15 party snacks

1 recipe choux pastry (see recipe for Cheese Aigrettes)
Beaten egg to glaze
Salt and freshly ground black pepper to taste
175g (6oz) cream cheese, at room temperature
5ml (1 tsp) tomato puree
15ml (1 tblsp) chopped chives
100g (4oz) lean cooked ham, chopped
25-50g (1-2oz) almond nibs

To Garnish:
Finely chopped fresh parsley.

Make the choux pastry exactly as directed for Cheese Aigrettes, but do not add the grated cheese. Season. Allow to cool.
Using a large piping bag and a 1cm (½ in) plain tube, pipe fingers of the choux paste about 2.5cm (1 in) long onto a greased baking sheet. Brush all over with the beaten egg. Sprinkle with the almond nibs. Bake on the top shelf of a pre-heated oven 200°C, 400°F, Gas Mark 6, for about 20 minutes, or until puffed up and golden.
Transfer to a cooling tray and immediately make a slit in the side of each with a sharp vegetable knife. This will allow the steam to escape. Allow to cool.
For the filling. Beat together the cream cheese, cream and tomato puree. Fold in the chives and ham. Season to taste.
Using a large piping bag fitted with 1cm (½ in) plain tube, or a teaspoon, fill the eclairs with the cream cheese mixture.
Serve immediately, sprinkled with the chopped parsley.
Note: The eclairs may be baked in the morning and left on the cooling tray until ready to fill.

Cheese Straws

PREPARATION TIME: 20-30 minutes

COOKING TIME: 15-20 minutes

MAKES: 18-20 party snacks

200g (8oz) plain flour
5ml (1 tsp) mustard powder
Salt and freshly ground black pepper to taste
Pinch of cayenne pepper
100g (4oz) butter
100g (4oz) mature Cheddar cheese, finely grated
1 egg yolk
Cold water to mix   mixed with
A little beaten egg

Sieve the flour, mustard powder, seasoning and cayenne pepper. Rub in the butter. Fork in the cheese. Mix to a stiff dough with the egg yolk and water.

Roll the pastry out to a thickness of 1 cm (½ in). Cut into straws about 10 cm (4 in) long. Cut out a pastry ring, using two plain cutters. Brush ring and straws with beaten egg.

Arrange on baking sheet and bake just above centre of a preheated oven 200°C, 400°F, Gas Mark 6, for 15-20 minutes, or until golden. Serve the cooled straws, stacked in the ring.

Smoked Salmon Flowers (right), Savoury Eclairs (centre right) and Cheese Straws (far right).

Smoked Salmon Flowers

PREPARATION TIME: 20-30 minutes

MAKES: 12 party snacks

175g (6oz) plain flour
75g (3oz) butter or margarine
2.5ml (½ tsp) salt
Cold water to bind
2 eggs, size 2
30ml (2 tblsp) milk
25g (1oz) butter
Salt and freshly ground black pepper to taste
15ml (1 tblsp) double cream
100g (4oz) thin slices smoked salmon

To Garnish:
A few chopped chives.

Make the patties. Sieve flour and salt. Rub in margarine. Mix to a firm dough with the water. Roll out and cut 12 rounds using a fluted cutter. Line 12 jam tart tins. Prick with a fork.

Bake blind on the second shelf of a pre-heated oven 200°C, 400°F, Gas Mark 6, for 10-15 minutes. Remove from tins and allow to cool.

Beat eggs and milk together, and season lightly. Melt butter in medium pan over low heat. Stir in egg mixture and cook over a low heat, stirring all the time until mixture scrambles. Remove from heat and allow to cool slightly, stirring. Stir in cream. Set aside to cool.

Cut smoked salmon into strips and line each pastry case. Top with a little of the cooled scrambled egg and garnish each salmon flower with a few chopped chives.

Sausage Toasties

PREPARATION TIME: 15-20 minutes

COOKING TIME: 20-30 minutes

MAKES: 24 party snacks

12 pork sausages, pricked
12 medium slices from a cut loaf
75g (3oz) butter
10ml (2 tsp) made mustard

Cut the crusts off the bread and roll each slice out flat with a rolling pin.
Stirring continuously, melt the butter and mustard together over a low heat. Brush each slice of bread with the melted mustard butter.
Roll each piece of prepared bread round a sausage to enclose completely. Cut in half to give 24 rolls.
Arrange on a baking sheet, join-side down, and bake on the second shelf of a pre-heated oven 170°C, 375°F, Gas Mark 5, for 20-30 minutes, until golden brown.
Serve hot or cold.

Stuffed Mushrooms

PREPARATION TIME: 20 minutes

COOKING TIME: 20 minutes

MAKES: 28 party snacks

60ml (4 tblsp) blue cheese
  mayonnaise
50g (2oz) cooked bacon, chopped
1 clove garlic, crushed
25g (1oz) fresh breadcrumbs
350g (12oz) button mushrooms,
  stalks removed
50g (2oz) butter

To Serve:
Croutons of toast.

Put the mayonnaise into a mixing bowl. Fold in the bacon, garlic and the breadcrumbs.
Melt the butter in a 25cm (10 in) flan dish in an oven preheated to 175°C, 350°F, Gas Mark 4. This will take about 7-10 minutes.
Fill the mushrooms, dark, gill side up, with the blue cheese mixture. Arrange in the hot butter. Using a pastry brush, carefully brush the butter round sides of each stuffed mushroom.
Bake, uncovered, for 10-15 minutes, then increase temperature to 190°C, 400°F, Gas Mark 6, for 5 minutes.
Serve, hot or cold, on the circles of toasted bread.

Asparagus Peanut Rolls

PREPARATION TIME: 20 minutes

MAKES: 14 party snacks

1 large brown loaf, uncut
50g (2oz) butter, at room temperature
10ml (2 tsp) smooth peanut butter
Few drops lemon juice
340g (12oz) can asparagus spears,
  drained

Garnish:
Lemon butterflies
Chicory leaves

Cut the crusts off the loaf.
Beat the peanut butter and lemon juice into the butter. Cut the bread thinly and roll each slice out flat with a rolling pin. Spread the bread with the flavoured butter and place a piece of drained asparagus on each piece of bread. Roll bread round asparagus to enclose completely. Trim asparagus stem if necessary.
Serve garnished with the lemon butterflies and chicory leaves.

Salami Open Sandwiches

PREPARATION TIME: 20 minutes

MAKES: 6 party snacks

6 slices rye bread
75g (3oz) cream cheese
18 slices of salami
A few drained asparagus tips
1 small onion, ringed
Slices of cucumber
1 Iceberg lettuce, shredded

Remove crusts and cut each slice of bread into an attractive shape. Spread thickly with cream cheese. Top with salami and decorate as required — see picture.
Serve on a bed of Iceberg lettuce.
Note: It will be necessary to use a knife and fork for this snack.

Asparagus Peanut Rolls (left), Stuffed Mushrooms (below left) and Sausage Toasties (bottom).

Cauliflower and Courgette Fritters

PREPARATION TIME: 30 minutes
COOKING TIME: 20-30 minutes
MAKES: 45 party snacks

175g (6oz) cauliflower florets
175g (6oz) baby courgettes

For the Fritter Batter:
150g (5oz) self-raising flour
2.5ml (½ tsp) salt
1 egg
135ml (5 fl oz) cold water

Top and tail the courgettes and cut into bite size pieces. Do not wash either the courgettes or cauliflower florets but wipe clean with a damp cloth if necessary.
Make the batter. Sieve the flour and salt into a mixing bowl. Make a well in the centre. Separate the egg, putting the yolk into the well in the flour and the white into a clean, medium-sized mixing bowl. Adding the water gradually, mix the flour and egg yolk to a smooth batter with a wooden spoon.
Whisk the egg white until standing in soft peaks and fold into the batter with a metal spoon.
Meanwhile, heat the oil in a deep fat fryer to 190°C (375°F). Dip the prepared vegetables into the batter to coat and then, using a slotted spoon, lower each piece of battered vegetable into the hot oil. Fry until crisp and golden.
Do not try to fry more than 8 pieces of vegetable at a time so that the temperature of the oil is maintained.
Drain on absorbent kitchen paper and serve piping hot accompanied by Seafood Dip (see recipe).

Cheese Aigrettes

PREPARATION TIME: 20-30 minutes
COOKING TIME: 30 minutes
MAKES: 25-27 party snacks

For the Choux Pastry:
150ml (¼ pint) cold water
50g (2oz) butter
65g (2½oz) plain flour
Salt and freshly ground pepper to taste
2 eggs, size 3, beaten

75g (3oz) grated Cheddar cheese
5ml (1 tsp) made mustard
Pinch cayenne pepper
Oil to deep fry

Put the water and butter into a medium saucepan. Bring the water to the boil. Stir to ensure butter has melted.
Turn off heat and immediately add the sifted flour and seasoning, all at once. Beat well with a wooden spoon until a ball of shiny dough results which leaves the side of the pan clean. Set aside for 5-10 minutes to cool slightly.
Gradually beat in the beaten eggs, a little at a time, until a thick, glossy paste results. Beat cheese, mustard and cayenne pepper into prepared choux pastry.
Meanwhile, heat the oil in a deep fat fryer to 190°C (375°F).
Fry teaspoons of the mixture in the deep fat until puffed up and golden brown. Do not fry more than 8 teaspoons of choux paste at a time so that the temperature of the oil is maintained.
Drain on absorbent kitchen paper and serve immediately.

Breaded Scampi

PREPARATION TIME: 20 minutes
COOKING TIME: 20-30 minutes
MAKES: 30 party snacks

450g (1lb) peeled Dublin Bay prawns, defrosted if frozen
1 egg, beaten
125-150g (4-5oz) fresh brown breadcrumbs
Oil to deep fry

Garnish:
Lemon wedges and fresh sprigs parsley

As an Accompaniment:
Tartare sauce

Blot the prawns as dry as possible on plenty of absorbent kitchen paper. This is particularly important if frozen prawns are used.
Put the beaten egg into a cereal bowl, and the breadcrumbs onto a dinner plate. Dip the prawns into the beaten egg and then in the breadcrumbs to coat. Repeat until all the prawns have been coated.
Meanwhile, heat the oil in the deep fat fryer to 375°F (190°C) and fry the prepared scampi, no more than 10 at a time, so that the temperature of the oil is maintained, until golden brown (about 5 minutes).
Drain on absorbent kitchen paper and serve hot, garnished with the lemon and parsley. Pass a bowl of tartare sauce round separately.

Cheese Aigrettes (left), Cauliflower and Courgette Fritters (below) and Breaded Scampi (bottom).

Cocktail Sausage Rolls with Apple

PREPARATION TIME: 30 minutes

COOKING TIME: about 20 minutes

MAKES: 30 party snacks

350g (12oz) packet frozen puff pastry, defrosted
450g (1lb) pork sausage meat
1 eating apple 100g (4oz) peeled, cored and chopped
Salt and freshly ground black pepper to taste
Flour
1 beaten egg

Roll the pastry out to a thickness of about 5mm (¼ in) and cut into 2 strips about 10cm (4 in) wide. Work the apple and seasoning into the sausage meat. Shape into two long rolls to fit the pastry. Dust sausage meat lightly with seasoned flour and arrange on each strip of pastry.

Brush the edges of each strip of pastry with beaten egg. Fold the pastry over and seal.

Using the back of a knife, knock up and then flute the edges. Make two slits with a sharp vegetable knife on the top of each roll at 1cm (½ in) intervals to allow the steam to escape.

Brush all over with beaten egg and cut into 2.5cm (1 in) pieces.

Arrange on a dampened baking sheet and bake just above centre in a pre-heated oven at 210°C, 450°F, Gas Mark 7, for about 20 minutes, or until golden brown. Best served warm.

Spiced Chilli Savouries (above), Cocktail Sausage Rolls with Apple (right) and Salami Open Sandwiches (far right).

Spiced Chilli Savouries

PREPARATION TIME: 20 minutes
COOKING TIME: 10 minutes
MAKES: 30 party snacks

300g (12oz) raw minced beef
50g (2oz) fresh brown breadcrumbs
1 small onion, finely chopped
10ml (2 tsp) finely chopped oregano
10ml (2 tsp) ground chilli powder
15ml (1 tblsp) tomato purée
10ml (2 tsp) made mustard
Salt and freshly ground pepper to taste

½ a beaten egg
Seasoned flour for coating
25-50g (1-2oz) garlic butter, melted

Put the beef into a large mixing bowl. Add the breadcrumbs, onion, oregano, chilli powder, tomato purée, mustard and the seasoning.
Mix well. Bind the mixture together with the beaten egg. Roll teaspoons of the mixture into small meat balls. Toss in the seasoned flour to coat.

Brush with the melted garlic butter and grill under a medium heat, turning occasionally until evenly browned.
Serve on cocktail sticks, accompanied by the mixed seafood dip (see recipe).
Note: This snack may be served hot or cold, but is best served within 2 hours of preparation.

Chinese Melon (top), Stuffed Vine Leaves (above) and Peach with Parma Ham (left).

Stuffed Vine Leaves

PREPARATION TIME: 20 minutes

COOKING TIME: 15 minutes

MAKES: 20-24 party snacks

225g (8oz) packet vine leaves
100g (4oz) cooked chicken meat,
　minced
100g (4oz) cooked lean lamb,
　minced
30ml (2 tblsp) cooked brown rice
2 spring onions, chopped
5ml (1 tsp) tarragon, finely chopped
30ml (2 tblsp) apple sauce
Salt and freshly ground black pepper
　to taste
30ml (2 tblsp) grape seed oil or corn
　oil
1 medium onion, chopped
30ml (2 tblsp) tomato puree
15ml (1 tblsp) dry white wine

Carefully dip the vine leaves into a
pan of boiling water. Drain well on
a clean tea towel.
Combine the minced chicken and
lamb, the rice, spring onions, the
tarragon and apple sauce. Mix
well. Season.
Put a small amount of the filling in
the centre of each drained vine
leaf. Roll up.
Put the oil into a large, shallow
frying pan. Heat for 1-2 minutes,
then fry the onion until soft but
not brown. Stir in the tomato
puree and wine. Season.
Stir in 30ml (2 tblsp) water. Lower
the stuffed vine leaves carefully
into the pan using a slotted spoon.
Cover with a lid and simmer
gently for 15 minutes, checking
after 5 minutes that there is
sufficient liquid.
Note: It will be necessary to use a
knife and fork with this dish,
which is delicious hot or cold.

Peach with Parma Ham

PREPARATION TIME: 20 minutes

MAKES: about 45 party snacks

2 large, ripe peaches
100g (4oz) Parma ham
Cocktail sticks

Peel the peaches—this is much
easier if the peaches are covered
with boiling water for 1-2 minutes
first.
Halve the peeled peaches and
remove the stone. Cut each half
into bite size pieces.

Cut the ham into thin strips and
roll one strip round each peach
piece. Secure with cocktail sticks.
Serve chilled.
Note: When fresh peaches are not
available, use drained, canned
pineapple pieces or cubes of fresh
melon.

Chinese Melon

PREPARATION TIME: 40 minutes

COOKING TIME: 10 minutes

SERVES: 8-10 people

350g (12oz) fillet of pork, cut into
　2.5cm (1 in) cubes
1 green or yellow melon, chilled
Oil for brushing
Salt and freshly ground black pepper
　to taste
425g (15oz) can pineapple pieces in
　natural juice, drained and juice
　reserved

For the Optional Dressing:

5ml (1 tsp) soya sauce
30ml (2 tblsp) pineapple juice
1 clove garlic, crushed
Pinch ground ginger
15ml (1 tblsp) white wine vinegar
30ml (2 tblsp) olive oil

Brush the cubes of pork with a
little oil. Season and thread onto
kebab sticks or meat skewers.
Grill under a medium grill,
turning occasionally until well
cooked. Set aside to cool.
Carefully cut the melon in half,
horizontally. Remove seeds and
discard. Remove melon flesh and
dice. Serrate the melon shells.
Fill the serrated melon shells with
the cooked pork cut into small
pieces, the diced melon flesh and
the pineapple pieces.
Put all the ingredients for the
dressing into a screw-top jar.
Screw on the lid. Shake to mix.
Arrange the filled melon on a
serving dish and, just before
serving, pour over the prepared
dressing, if using. Serve
immediately with cocktail sticks.

Fish Kebabs

PREPARATION TIME: 15 minutes

COOKING TIME: 10 minutes

MAKES: 6 party snacks

350g (12oz) boneless cod, cubed
225g (8oz) large, peeled prawns
225g (8oz) lamb's liver, cut into pieces
225g (8oz) can pineapple rings
 drained and cut into pieces
50g (2oz) butter
1 clove garlic, crushed
5ml (1 tsp) finely chopped fresh parsley
6 bridge rolls
Butter for spreading (optional)
6 metal meat skewers

Load each skewer with alternating pieces of the prepared food; that is, a cube of cod, a prawn, a piece of lamb's liver and a piece of pineapple until each skewer is full. Put the butter, garlic and parsley into a small pan and set over a low heat, stirring until the butter has melted.
Brush the kebabs all over with the garlic butter, and grill, turning occasionally, until well cooked. Split the bridge rolls and butter if required. Slip the food off the kebab sticks into the prepared rolls.
Serve immediately with a choice of relish.

Crab Rounds

PREPARATION TIME: 20 minutes

MAKES: 16 party snacks

2 cucumbers, ends removed
170g (6oz) can crab meat
95g (3½oz) can pink salmon, skin
 and bones removed
60ml (4 tblsp) double cream, whipped
5ml (1 tsp) tomato purée
5ml (1 tsp) lemon juice
Salt and freshly ground black pepper
 to taste

Garnish:
Slices of pimento olives
Parsley

Cut both the cucumbers evenly into 8 large rings. Using a teaspoon, hollow out a boat in each ring, leaving a shell 5mm (¼ in) thick. Sprinkle with salt and leave them to stand upside down while preparing filling.
In a mixing bowl combine the drained, chopped crab meat, the drained, flaked salmon, the cream,

tomato purée, lemon juice and seasoning to taste. Rinse cucumber rings and blot dry.
Fill each prepared cucumber boat with the crab mixture.
Garnish with a slice of pimento olive and a tiny piece of parsley before serving.
Note: If liked, the cucumber boats may be crimped as in the picture, before hollowing out. This is rather time-consuming, however.

Mixed Seafood Dip

PREPARATION TIME: 15 minutes

SERVES: 8 people

100g (4oz) large, cooked, peeled
 prawns
100g (4oz) smoked salmon
100g (4oz) lobster meat

For the Dip:
300ml (5fl oz) soured cream
75g (3oz) Stilton cheese, crumbled
15ml (1 tblsp) natural yoghurt
45ml (3 tblsp) mayonnaise
5ml (1 tsp) fresh basil, finely chopped
5ml (1 tsp) lemon juice
1-2 cloves garlic, crushed (optional)
Salt and freshly ground black pepper
 to taste

To Accompany:
Strips of peeled carrot
Strips of cucumber, peel left on

Prepare the dip. Put the soured cream into a mixing bowl. Stir in the Stilton, yoghurt, mayonnaise, basil, lemon juice, garlic if used, and seasoning to taste. Mix well. Transfer the dip to an attractive serving dish, set in the centre of a large plate.
Put the seafood in groups around the dish of dip, leaving the prawns whole, cutting the lobster meat into bite-sized pieces and making the smoked salmon into rolls, secured with cocktail sticks. Add the sticks of carrot and cucumber and serve immediately.
Note: This recipe may be prepared on the morning or the party but keep covered with cling film in the refrigerator until ready to serve.

**Crab Rounds (right), Mixed Seafood
Dip (below) and Fish Kebabs (bottom).**

For anyone preferring not to drink alcohol, the following drinks succeed on three counts: they tempt the eye, they tempt the palate and they taste delicious. The Pussyfoot (far left) not only tastes good, but it is healthy too, combining orange, lemon and lime juices with egg yolk and grenadine (which adds sweetness and colour) and, here, it is made into a long drink by topping up the glass with soda water. A Jersey Lily (second from left) is basically fizzy apple juice with a dash of Angostura bitters, and the San Francisco (third from left) is another of the refreshing fruit juice and grenadine concoctions. Ice cream, fresh cream and cola add up to a Mickey Mouse (centre front), while the Capucine (third from right) is another creamy mixture, this time flavoured with peppermint and topped with grated chocolate. The Princess Margaret (second from right) is virtually a strawberry sorbet, served in a sugar-frosted glass, the rim of the glass dipped in sirop de fraise and then in granulated sugar. The marzipan-like taste of the Yellow Dwarf (far right) comes from orgeat – a non-alcoholic, almond-flavoured syrup.

MOCKTAILS

'Temperance is the noblest gift of the gods' (Euripides), and 'Temperance is the greatest of all the virtues' (Plutarch). And who are we to argue? Syrups in flavours as diverse as peach, almond, strawberry and mint, as well as a wide range of exotic fruit juices mean that mocktails can be just as exciting and delicious as their alcoholic rivals. Here is the chance to go a little bit mad with the garnishes – so let your imagination run riot!

ACAPULCO GOLD

Shake together six parts pineapple juice, one part grapefruit juice, two parts coconut cream, two parts fresh cream and a scoop of crushed ice. Serve unstrained.

ANITA

Shake together three parts orange juice, one part lemon juice and a couple of dashes of Angostura bitters. Top with soda water, garnish with fruit and serve with straws.

APPLEADE

Chop up two large apples and pour a pint of boiling water over them. Sprinkle in about a teaspoon of sugar and leave to stand for a few minutes. Strain the liquid and leave to cool. Serve with plenty of ice and garnish with a wedge of apple and a slice of lemon.

BARLEYADE

Pour equal quantities of lemon barley and lemonade into a tumbler; add ice, a slice of lemon, and straws.

BOO BOO'S SPECIAL

Shake together equal quantities of orange juice and pineapple juice, a squeeze of lemon juice, a dash of Angostura bitters, a dash of grenadine and a scoop of crushed ice. Serve unstrained, garnish with fruit and top with a little water if desired.

CAPUCINE

Shake together one part peppermint cordial and four parts fresh cream. Strain and add crushed ice. Finely grate a little plain chocolate over the top.

CINDERELLA

Shake together equal parts pineapple juice, orange juice and lemon juice. Strain over ice cubes, top with soda water and splash in a little grenadine. Garnish with a slice of pineapple, or a pineapple chunk and a cherry on a stick, and serve with straws.

EGG NOG

Shake together a tumbler-full of milk, an egg, a teaspoon of sugar and ice. Dust with freshly-grated nutmeg, garnish with a maraschino cherry and serve with straws.

GODCHILD

Place four or five ice cubes in the glass and fill three-quarters full with lemonade. Add a squeeze of lemon juice and gently pour a measure of sirop de cassis on top. Garnish with a slice of lemon and serve with straws.

GRECIAN

Blend together four parts peach juice, two parts orange juice, one part lemon juice and a scoop of crushed ice. Pour unstrained into the glass, add a squirt of soda water and garnish with fresh fruit.

(Above) Egg Nog, Capucine, Saint Clements, Queen Charlie, Lemonade Golden and (facing page) Nursery Fizz

JERSEY LILY

Stir a glass of fizzy apple juice with a little sugar, a dash of Angostura bitters and ice cubes. Strain and garnish with a maraschino cherry.

KEELPLATE

Shake together two parts tomato juice, one part clam juice, a couple of dashes of Worcestershire sauce and a good pinch of celery salt.

LEMONADE (FIZZY)

Pour the juice of a lemon into the glass and add two teaspoons of sugar. Stir until the sugar is dissolved, add four or five ice cubes and top up with soda water. Garnish with a slice of lemon.

LEMONADE (GOLDEN)

Shake together the juice of a lemon, a wine-glass of water, an egg yolk and two teaspoons of sugar. Strain into the glass, add ice cubes and garnish with fruit.

LEMONADE (PINK)

Make in the same way as still lemonade

(below) and stir in a tablespoon of sirop de framboise.

LEMONADE (STILL)

Shake together two scoops of crushed ice, the juice of a lemon and two teaspoons of sugar. Pour, unstrained, into the glass and top up with water. Garnish with a slice of lemon and serve with straws.

LEMON ICE CREAM SODA

Put two tablespoons of fresh lemon juice in a glass with two teaspoons of sugar and stir until the sugar is dissolved. Fill the glass two-thirds full with soda water and top with a large scoop of soft vanilla ice cream. Serve with straws and a spoon. Similarly, orange or grapefruit versions can be made.

LIMEADE

Shake together the juice of three limes and sugar to taste. Strain over ice cubes and add water or soda water. Garnish with fruit.

LIMEY

Shake together two parts lime juice, one part lemon juice and half an egg white. Garnish with a cherry.

MICKEY MOUSE

Over ice cubes pour cola, then add a scoop of soft vanilla ice cream, top with whipped cream and two cherries, and serve with straws and a spoon.

MOCK DAISY CRUSTA

Put two scoops of crushed ice into the glass and add the juice of two limes and a tablespoon of sirop de framboise. Top up with soda water and float a little grenadine on top. Garnish with a sprig of mint and raspberries on a stick.

NURSERY FIZZ

Over ice cubes pour equal parts orange juice and ginger ale. Garnish with a slice of orange and a cherry and serve with straws.

PRINCESS MARGARET

Blend together five or six strawberries, a slice of pineapple, the juice of half a lemon, juice of half an orange, a couple of dashes of sirop de fraise and a scoop of crushed ice. Pour into a sugar-frosted glass (stick the sugar with sirop de fraise rather than egg white or gomme), and garnish with a strawberry on the rim.

PUSSYFOOT

Shake together equal parts orange juice, lemon juice and lime juice, along with a dash of grenadine and an egg yolk. Add soda water if desired, garnish with a cherry and serve with straws.

QUEEN CHARLIE

Over ice cubes pour a measure of grenadine and top up with soda water. Garnish with a slice of lemon and a cherry on a stick, and serve with straws.

SAINT CLEMENTS

The name derives from the children's nursery rhyme "Oranges and lemons say the bells of Saint Clements…" and the drink is made by stirring equal parts of orange juice and bitter lemon with plenty of ice.

Americano (above) and Acapulco Gold (facing page)

Serve garnished with slices of orange and lemon.

SAN FRANCISCO

Shake together equal parts orange juice, lemon juice, grapefruit juice and pineapple juice, along with an egg white and a dash of grenadine. Top up with soda water and garnish extravagantly!

SHIRLEY TEMPLE

Over ice cubes pour ginger ale and add a little grenadine. Stir and garnish with a cherry.

SOUTHERN BELLE

A non-alcoholic Mint Julep…Crush a sprig of mint with a teaspoon of sugar at the bottom of a glass, to extract the mint flavour. Add a squeeze of lemon juice and lots of ice. Top up with ginger ale, garnish with a sprig of mint and serve with straws.

SUMMERTIME SODA

Stir the juice of an orange with the juice of a lemon and the juice of a grapefruit. Pour over ice cubes and add soda water and a

scoop of soft vanilla ice cream. Serve with straws and a spoon.

SURFER'S PARADISE

Over ice cubes pour the juice of half a lime and three dashes of Angostura bitters. Stir in lemonade to top up and garnish with a slice of orange.

TOMATO JUICE COCKTAIL

Shake together tomato juice, a good squeeze of lemon juice, a couple of dashes of Worcestershire sauce, a couple of drops of Tabasco, a pinch of celery salt and a shake of pepper. Strain and serve straight up or on the rocks. Garnish with a slice of lemon and a stick of celery.

YELLOW DWARF

Shake together one part orgeat syrup, one part cream and an egg yolk. Strain and add soda water to taste. Garnish with a maraschino cherry.

Prevention, as the saying goes, is better than cure…It is also less painful. A glass of milk and preferably a meal taken before you start drinking lines the stomach and protects against too harsh an onslaught. However, if you do wake up wishing you hadn't, knock back one of these monsters, and you may feel instantly revitalised. I do not necessarily guarantee their efficacy.

BULLSHOT

Shake together one part vodka, four parts condensed consommé or beef bouillon, a couple of dashes of Worcestershire sauce, a dash of lemon juice and a pinch of celery salt. Add Tabasco and pepper to taste.

CORPSE REVIVER COCKTAIL

Shake together one part brandy, four parts milk, a teaspoon of sugar or gomme syrup and a dash of Angostura bitters. Top up with soda water.

PICK-ME-UP

Stir one part cognac with one part pastis and one part dry vermouth.

PRAIRIE HEN

Into a small goblet pour a couple of dashes of vinegar and two teaspoons of Worcestershire sauce. Carefully break a

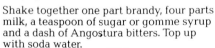

Prairie Oyste

whole egg into the glass without breaking the yolk, sprinkle with pepper and salt, and splash with a little Tabasco. Drink in one gulp.

PRAIRIE OYSTER

Into a small tumbler pour a teaspoon of Worcestershire sauce and a teaspoon of tomato sauce. Stir, and then gently add a whole, unbroken egg yolk. Splash with a little vinegar and dust with pepper. Drink i one gulp.

INDEX